China's Future

China's Future

FOREIGN POLICY AND ECONOMIC DEVELOPMENT IN THE POST-MAO ERA

ALLEN S. WHITING

ROBERT F. DERNBERGER

Introduction by Bayless Manning

1980s Project/Council on Foreign Relations

McGRAW-HILL BOOK COMPANY

New York   St. Louis   San Francisco
Auckland   Bogotá   Düsseldorf   Johannesburg   London   Madrid
Mexico   Montreal   New Delhi   Panama   Paris   São Paulo
Singapore   Sydney   Tokyo   Toronto

The Council on Foreign Relations, Inc. is a nonprofit and nonpartisan organization devoted to promoting improved understanding of international affairs through the free exchange of ideas. Its membership of about 1,700 persons throughout the United States is made up of individuals with special interest and experience in international affairs. The Council has no affiliation with and receives no funding from the United States government.

The Council publishes the quarterly journal *Foreign Affairs* and, from time to time, books and monographs which in the judgment of the Council's Committee on Studies are responsible treatments of significant international topics worthy of presentation to the public. The 1980s Project is a research effort of the Council; as such, 1980s Project Studies have been similarly reviewed through procedures of the Committee on Studies. As in the case of all Council publications, statements of fact and expressions of opinion contained in 1980s Project Studies are the sole responsibility of their authors.

The editor of this book was Michael Schwarz for the Council on Foreign Relations. Thomas Quinn and Michael Hennelly were the editors for McGraw-Hill Book Company. Christopher Simon was the designer and Milton J. Heiberg supervised the production. This book was set in Times Roman by Creative Book Services, Inc.

Printed and bound by R. R. Donnelley & Sons.

Library of Congress Cataloging in Publication Data

Whiting, Allen Suess
China's future.

(1980s project/Council on Foreign Relations)
Includes bibliographies and index.
1. China—Foreign relations—1976- 2. China—
Politics and government—1976- 3. China—
Economic conditions—1949- I. Dernberger, Robert F.,
joint author. II. Title. III. Series: Council on
Foreign Relations. 1980s project/Council on Foreign
Relations.
DS777.55.W44   327.51   77-4358
ISBN 0-07-069958-5
ISBN 0-07-069959-3 pbk.

2 3 4 5 6 7 8 9 R R D R R D 7 0 9 8

Contents

Foreword: The 1980s Project

These studies of the likely course of China's foreign policy and the evolution of its economy are part of a stream of studies to be produced in the course of the 1980s Project of the Council on Foreign Relations. Each 1980s Project study analyzes an issue or set of issues that is likely to be of international concern during the next 10 to 20 years.

The ambitious purpose of the 1980s Project is to examine important political and economic problems not only individually but in relationship to one another. Some studies or books produced by the Project will primarily emphasize the interrelationship of issues. In the case of other, more specifically focused studies, a considerable effort has been made to write, review, and criticize them in the context of more general Project work. Each Project study is thus capable of standing on its own; at the same time it has been shaped by a broader perspective.

The 1980s Project had its origins in the widely held recognition that many of the assumptions, policies, and institutions that have characterized international relations during the past 30 years are inadequate to the demands of today and the foreseeable demands of the period between now and 1990 or so. Over the course of the next decade, substantial adaptation of institutions and behavior will be needed to respond to the changed circumstances of the 1980s and beyond. The Project seeks to identify those future conditions and the kinds of adaptation they might require. It is not the Project's purpose to arrive at a single or exclusive set of goals.

Nor does it focus upon the foreign policy or national interests of the United States alone. Instead, it seeks to identify goals that are compatible with the perceived interests of most states, despite differences in ideology and in level of economic development.

The published products of the Project are aimed at a broad readership, including policy makers and potential policy makers and those who would influence the policy-making process, but are confined to no single nation or region. The authors of Project studies were therefore asked to remain mindful of interests broader than those of any one society and to take fully into account the likely realities of domestic politics in the principal societies involved. All those who have worked in the Project, however, have tried not to be captives of the status quo; they have sought to question the inevitability of existing patterns of thought and behavior that restrain desirable change and to look for ways in which those patterns might in time be altered or their consequences mitigated.

The 1980s Project is at once a series of separate attacks upon a number of urgent and potentially urgent international problems and also a collective effort, involving a substantial number of persons in the United States and abroad, to bring those separate approaches to bear upon one another and to suggest the kinds of choices that might be made among them. The Project involves more than 300 participants. A small central staff and a steering Coordinating Group have worked to define the questions and to assess the compatibility of policy prescriptions. Nearly 100 authors, from more than a dozen countries, have been at work on separate studies. Ten working groups of specialists and generalists have been convened to subject the Project's studies to critical scrutiny and to help in the process of identifying interrelationships among them.

The 1980s Project is the largest single research and studies effort the Council on Foreign Relations has undertaken in its 55-year history, comparable in conception only to a major study of the postwar world, the War and Peace Studies, undertaken by the Council during the Second World War. At that time, the impetus to the effort was the discontinuity caused by worldwide conflict and visible and inescapable need to rethink, replace, and supplement many of the features of the international system that had prevailed before the war. The discontinuities in today's world are less obvious and, even when occasionally quite visible—as in the abandonment of gold convertibility and fixed monetary parities—only briefly command the spotlight of public attention. That new institutions and patterns of behavior are needed in many areas is widely acknowledged, but the sense of need is less urgent—existing institutions have not for the most part dramatically failed and collapsed. The tendency, therefore, is to make do with outmoded arrangements and to improvise rather than to undertake a basic analysis of the problems that lie before us and of the demands that those problems will place upon all nations.

The 1980s Project is based upon the belief that serious effort and integrated forethought can contribute—indeed, are indispensable—to progress in the next decade toward a more humane, peaceful, productive, and just world. And it rests upon the hope that participants in its deliberations and readers of Project publications—whether or not they agree with an author's point of view—may be helped to think more informedly about the opportunities and the dangers that lie ahead and the consequences of various possible courses of future action.

The 1980s Project has been made possible by generous grants from the Ford Foundation, the Lilly Endowment, the Andrew W. Mellon Foundation, the Rockefeller Foundation, and the German Marshall Fund of the United States. Neither the Council on Foreign Relations nor any of those foundations is responsible for statements of fact and expressions of opinion contained in publications of the 1980s Project; they are the sole responsibility of the individual authors under whose names they appear. But the Council on Foreign Relations and the staff of the 1980s Project take great pleasure in placing those publications before a wide readership both in the United States and abroad.

Richard H. Ullman
Director, the 1980s Project

xi

During 1975 and 1976, ten Working Groups met to explore major international issues and to subject initial drafts of 1980s Project studies to critical review. Those who chaired Project Working Groups were:

Cyrus R. Vance, Working Group on Nuclear Weapons and Other Weapons of Mass Destruction

Leslie H. Gelb, Working Group on Armed Conflict

Roger Fisher, Working Group on Transnational Violence and Subversion

Rev. Theodore M. Hesburgh, Working Group on Human Rights

Joseph S. Nye, Jr., Working Group on the Political Economy of North-South Relations

Harold Van B. Cleveland, Working Group on Macroeconomic Policies and International Monetary Relations

Lawrence C. McQuade, Working Group on Principles of International Trade

William Diebold, Jr., Working Group on Multinational Enterprises

Eugene B. Skolnikoff, Working Group on the Environment, the Global Commons, and Economic Growth

Miriam Camps, Working Group on Industrial Policy

The members of the 1980s Project staff are:

Miriam Camps   *Catherine Gwin*
William Diebold, Jr.   *Roger Hansen*
David C. Gompert   *Edward L. Morse*
           Richard H. Ullman (Director)

The Committee on Studies of the Board of Directors of the Council on Foreign Relations was the governing body of the 1980s Project. The Committee's members as of December 31, 1976 were:

W. Michael Blumenthal   Walter J. Levy
Zbigniew Brzezinski   Joseph S. Nye, Jr.
Robert A. Charpie   Robert V. Roosa
Richard N. Cooper   Carroll L. Wilson
James A. Perkins (Chairman)

The Coordinating Group of the 1980s Project had a central advisory role in the work of the Project. Its members as of December 31, 1976 were:

W. Michael Blumenthal   Theodore R. Marmor
Richard N. Cooper   Ali Mazrui
Carlos F. Diaz-Alejandro   Joseph S. Nye, Jr.
Richard A. Falk   Michael O'Neill
Edward K. Hamilton   Marshall D. Shulman
Stanley Hoffmann   Stephen Stamas
Samuel P. Huntington   Fritz Stern
Gordon J. MacDonald   Allen S. Whiting
Bruce K. MacLaury
Bayless Manning (Chairman)

China's Future

Introduction: China in the 1980s

Bayless Manning

This volume in the series of 1980s Project studies is devoted entirely to the People's Republic of China. It contains two essays, one on the underlying elements that make for continuity in the economic development of China in the coming decade and one on its likely foreign policies in the same period. The mind-whirling swings of recent Chinese politics make even short-term forecasts about China hazardous, and long-range projection of the sort undertaken in this volume is a game for the most venturesome only. But the authors are brave men as well as able scholars.

Of course the political economy of modern China can be understood only in the context of its unique ancient cultural history, its battering at the hands of Europeans during its period of nineteenth-century weakness, and its 40 years of civil strife and foreign invasion during this century. But it was not part of the commission of Professors Dernberger and Whiting to write that history, and they have done what they were charged to do by the 1980s Project—to analyse prospectively. Their essays seek to explore the conditions that are likely to determine the range of Chinese policy choices during the coming decade or so and to speculate, in an informed way, about what those policies and their consequences are likely to be.

In two respects, these two essays are not typical of the 1980s Project series. First, they are addressed to a single country, whereas most of the Project's work is addressed to functional problems that will confront the international system within the next 10 or 15 years.*

Second, these essays on China are essentially descriptive and projective, rather than policy-oriented and normative as are most 1980s studies. But China is a special case calling for special treatment. Its sheer mass, with one-fourth of the earth's inhabitants, demands attention. Moreover, if its leadership is willing to sustain the costs, China is able to function largely independently of the global system, and it is questionable whether the course of China's policy can be significantly influenced by foreign policies (short of war) pursued by other countries. For generations China has been, as it is today, mainly a condition in the world's system—more a state of affairs than an assertive actor. Since that situation may well continue, China must be viewed as a separate entity as well as a part of the international system.

Yet, regardless of the extent to which China remains more a condition than an assertive actor, China's policy choices will clearly be of interest and of concern to other societies. At the outset of this volume, therefore, it is useful to suggest some of the principal questions regarding China's relations with other governments and institutions which readers might keep in mind as they consider these analyses by Professors Dernberger and Whiting. The "answers" provided by China's future policies with regard to each of these matters will ultimately help to shape the political and economic environment of the 1980s.

China and the Soviet Union Where will China and the U.S.S.R. locate themselves in the 1980s along the spectrum between war and entente? Geographically condemned to share a 4,000-mile border and ideologically self-condemned to contend for the papacy of international communism, both the Chinese and the Soviets must assign primary importance to their relationship. In turn, the character of that relationship is of major significance to the rest of the world. The global balance of power would be

*Another Project volume will focus on the Soviet Union in the 1980s. The U.S.S.R. will be the subject of a country study because the relationship between the United States and the Soviet Union, the two powers that are militarily "super," has a special importance to the entire international system.

2

substantially destabilized if Moscow and Peking should make common cause; the peace and security of the world might also be threatened if these two nuclear powers should be drawn into direct military conflict. From the perspective of the rest of the world, the present Sino-Soviet relationship of determined but nonbelligerent competition is probably the most desirable arrangement that can be hoped for.

Is there anything that countries other than the Soviet Union and China can do to affect the course of development of that relationship? The answer, probably, is very little. Overtly hostile behavior toward the People's Republic by the Western world, particularly the United States, could perhaps induce the Chinese to move to a friendlier relationship with the Soviets, but that result would advantage none but the Soviet Union. On the other hand, an accommodating Western policy toward the Chinese would likely do little to deter Peking from moving toward a more cordial relationship with the Kremlin if the Chinese leaders were to decide in favor of that course.

China and Japan   China and Japan have striking economic complementarities and share certain elements of cultural history that could provide the basis for a closer relationship. At the same time, profound suspicions and policy considerations on both sides tend to inhibit such a development. Japan is an anomaly in that it is the world's third largest economy but is wholly dependent upon the United States for its national security. A Japan that becomes unsure of United States support and apprehensive of the Soviet Union's growing naval power in the Pacific might, in spite of the ensuing domestic clamor, simultaneously move toward rearmament, a closer relationship with China, and an increase of the distance between itself and the other industrialized democracies. In turn, the evolution of relationships between China and Japan will significantly affect the rate of China's economic development and the orientation of Japan's future economic investment and expansion.

China and Its Other Neighbors   Apart from the Soviet Union and Japan, China must carry on some form of working relationship with the countries on its borders from Korea to India and with the other countries of Southeast Asia. Korea will likely prove to be a delicate and potentially dangerous political sore spot in the world for some time to come, as the interests of the divided Korean people, the Soviet Union, China, Japan, and the United States intersect there. A Sino-Soviet battle for influence is under way in virtually every capital of Asia, and canny local leaders, particularly in North Korea and Vietnam, persist in asserting their own independence and in playing Moscow against Peking. The thorny issue of Taiwan will also continue into the 1980s, no matter how the United States works out its own relationships with Peking and Taipei.

The People's Republic of China will almost certainly come into conflict with some of its neighbors and near-neighbors over oil and other mineral resources lying under the continental shelf of the South China Sea. Furthermore, one thread in the tapestry of Chinese politics has been the impulse to support leftist insurrection in other countries, particularly those that are within easy logistical reach of China. Yet the members of the Association of Southeast Asian Nations (ASEAN) are determined to pursue their own futures, free of Peking's domination and relatively free of economic and professional influence by the large numbers of overseas Chinese within their own borders. The existence of these large, locally unpopular Chinese minorities will further complicate China's relationships with its Asian neighbors and near-neighbors.

China and the West   To what extent will China accept the risks of increased dependence that would likely accompany a significant expansion of its economic and other relationships with the Western industrialized countries? What balance will it strike between a strategy of economic development that draws upon infusions of technology from abroad and a strategy that emphasizes "self-reliance?" That issue is an old one for China. Today it is the most important political issue in the country, over which top leaders of the party and state have risen and been destroyed. The evolving policy that emerges from day-to-day struggles over this issue will largely shape China's relationships with the institutional system and the economic system of the world.

China and the Third World   The People's Republic frequently seeks to present itself as the leader of the countries of the world that are poor, economically developing, nonwhite, and disadvantaged in the wake of European colonialism. International communism remains to a degree evangelical, and Peking sees itself as the propagator of the true faith. Moreover, with a pride that is on some points quite justified, the Chinese like to point to their system of economic development as a model for other developing nations. Few seriously believe that the Chinese model is wholly exportable to non-Chinese cultures, but the Chinese have already shown that they can be helpful in working on, and transferring the necessary skills for, certain projects in other developing countries. If Peking were to prove willing, over a period of years, to allocate the resources and incur the political costs of aggressively pursuing these political and economic roles in the Third World, and if it were to be even partially successful in doing so, the rest of the world could witness a spreading Chinese involvement and increasing Chinese political leverage in many parts of the Third World. Since the Soviet Union, the Western industrialized democracies, and the governments of many developing countries would all find such a development unwelcome, any Chinese efforts of this sort can be expected to set up reactive vibrations that could substantially alter the familiar alliance relationships and affinities of today's world.

China and the Global Institutional System   To what extent will China play an active or passive role vis-à-vis international institutions and internationally accepted norms of behavior? For example, when, if ever, will Peking consider that it has an interest in, and should take part in, shaping arms control agreements, international food programs, the law of the sea, the international monetary system, etc.? And if the People's Republic does begin to participate actively in such forums, will it do so with an eye toward collective problem solving or the aim of maintaining long-term confrontation and obstruction?

* * * * *

5

How much freedom will any governing Chinese regime have to choose its policies with regard to these six questions? If China does not maintain a rate of economic growth that exceeds its rate of population growth and meets the pressures of domestic expectations, it will not have much room for international maneuver and will be forced to do things it would prefer not to do. Necessity may be the mother of invention, but it is also the assassin of options. Moreover, if China is to play any major world role, the regime must maintain the elements of domestic political strength it has worked so long and so hard to achieve—national unity, administrative coherence, general public support, and a continuing capacity to motivate the people to work. If these conditions can be met, then the Chinese will have leeway to debate and effectively act upon China's ancient question of balance: how much to go out from and how much to stay at home in the Middle Kingdom.

Whether or not things go well for it and whether rich or poor, China can be expected to be an activist on matters that are at its doorstep and that directly concern its perceived interests. Dramatic illustrations were afforded by China's intervention in Korea in 1950 and by its active but carefully modulated support of North Vietnam throughout the entire course of the Indochina struggle. But even if a satisfactory rate of economic development and a continuation of basic political stability are achieved, will China in the future choose to participate more generally in the world's political and economic institutions? To a degree greater than any other country, China has the resources, the skills, the population, and—most important—the cultural heritage and security of attitude that enable it to see itself as the sun and the rest of the world's nations as planets. China's international relationships in any of the six areas listed earlier could have a major impact upon the politics of the rest of the world, but the reader will also want to consider carefully the possibility that China's course of development may prove largely external to the international problems of the 1980s. The role of China in international politics and economics may, despite its massive scale, turn out to be essentially peripheral and rhetorical.

For reasons that are difficult to reconstruct plausibly, the

United States for 20 years based its policies toward the People's Republic of China on a badly distorted picture of events in that country, of the implications of those events, and of China's relationship with its neighbors. As we now look forward into the coming decade, we must do a better job of getting the actual situation straight in our minds. That cannot be done by reading this volume alone, but these essays of Professors Dernberger and Whiting make an impressive contribution to understanding China today and China tomorrow.

China and the World

Allen S. Whiting

Introduction

The death of Mao Tse-tung in 1976 marked the end of an era in the life of the People's Republic of China (PRC). Not since the birth of the new regime in 1949, after 40 years of political and military turmoil, had so momentous an event confronted observers of China. In attempting to assess the likely course of Peking's foreign policy over the next decade, it is useful to recall how limited was the ability of observers in 1949 to forecast the developments of subsequent decades.

Initially the world watched with curiosity as the peasant armies of Mao Tse-tung established their rule over the largest civilization on earth. Alarming prognoses in 1949 predicted that Mao's strategy of acquiring power through armed struggle in the countryside would be spread throughout Asia by Peking's disciplined cadres and armed forces. One year later this possibility was enlarged to include the threat of open aggression when Chinese armies hurled the forces of General Douglas MacArthur's UN Command back from the Yalu River.

The next quarter-century, however, revealed the shortcomings of the prognoses and perceptions of 1949. Between 1949 and 1976 the Chinese Communists restored China's prestige and power, but not by spreading Mao's strategy through Asia. Even when that strategy proved successful in Indochina, Ho Chi Minh's mobilization of nationalism against the French was more important than Chinese assistance. While most observers warned of the threat posed by a Sino-Soviet bloc seemingly manifest in the

11

military alliance between Moscow and Peking concluded in February 1950, a few foresaw tension between China and the Soviet Union. None, however, predicted that despite being dependent on the Soviet Union for economic and military development, Mao would challenge Khrushchev in 1960 on ideological and political issues. Nor did many forecast that nine years later, bloody clashes would erupt on the Sino-Soviet border amidst general alarm over the prospect of a larger war between the two communist giants.

This record should deflate exaggerated expectations over the likelihood of complete success in any attempt to predict China's political evolution during the next 10 to 15 years. This particular effort begins, therefore, with a discussion of the problems inherent in forecasting Peking's policies following the death of Mao. This discussion is intended to delineate where our knowledge ends and reasonable speculation begins, thereby permitting unlikely contingencies to be excluded from consideration and narrowing the range of probable developments that need to be considered. The new mix of leadership is examined as a critical factor in China's political evolution because of the absence both of Mao Tse-tung, who played a unique role, and of consistent and institutionalized patterns of decision making. Leadership will also affect China's economic development, which is related to foreign policy both through decisions concerning reliance on foreign technology and through the impact of economic growth on military power. Economic factors are then briefly reviewed; they are analyzed much more extensively in the accompanying essay by Robert Dernberger. The chapter closes with discussion of those issues and choices that are likely to pose unavoidable problems to the post-Mao leadership, principally in foreign policy but often linked to or dependent upon domestic policy.

The Chinese vision of world affairs is then examined in order to assess the construct of ends and means that emerges from the compound of ideology, precedent, and the dynamic interaction of theory and practice that is a cardinal feature of Mao's precepts. This analysis provides a foundation for forecasting the likely range of Chinese policy choices regarding selected issues. However, these issues are chosen according to their interest to observers of China, not primarily from China's own perspective of its policy priorities. China's own possible and likely courses of action concerning matters such as international nuclear and conventional arms proliferation, armed intervention and subversion, and ocean resources are then discussed. This survey has modest aims: it is intended only to correct some misconceptions and offer some insights that will facilitate a fuller understanding of these selected issues. As such, it is only a partial introduction to the complexities and dynamics that will determine China's role in the world over the coming years.

ONE

Problems of Forecasting

Although China is the oldest society on earth, the People's Republic is the youngest regime among the major powers. As such, its institutions are more influenced by changes in leadership, as with the death of Mao, than those of long established governments. China also has the most backward and impoverished economy of the major states except for India. Thus its rulers may have greater impact on economic growth and the resultant military power that affects foreign affairs than is true in more advanced economies that are less immediately manipulable by policy makers or disrupted by policy error. These factors make assessments of the leadership composition and its implications for foreign policy uniquely important.

LEADERSHIP AND POLICY

For nearly 20 years Liu Shao-ch'i was the obvious successor to Mao Tse-tung, founder of the People's Republic. Then in 1966-67 Liu fell, denounced as "China's Khrushchev" and accused of plotting to "restore capitalism." In 1969 Lin Piao won formal designation as heir to the Chairman's mantle. Two years later Chinese officials claimed that Lin died in an airplane accident while attempting to flee to the Soviet Union after an abortive attempt on the Chairman's life. From 1973 to 1976 Teng Hsiao-p'ing rocketed upward in prominence and power after having earlier suffered political denunciation, along with Liu Shao-ch'i, as a "capitalist roader." However, following the death in January 1976 of Chou En-lai, Premier since 1949 and patron of Teng, the latter disappeared from sight amid fresh accusations of ideological subversion.

Then one month after Mao's death on September 9, 1976, a dramatic purge rocked Chinese politics with shock waves analogous to those that had accompanied the devastating earthquake earlier that summer. Official media announced that a "gang of four" had attempted to seize power, and mass demonstrations denounced the alleged culprits: Chiang Ch'ing, Mao's wife; Chang Ch'un-ch'iao, Deputy Premier and top political commissar in the People's Liberation Army (PLA); Wang Hun-wen, second-ranking Party leader; and Yao Wen-yuan, chief Party ideologue and propagandist. All four were Politburo members, catapulted to power in the Cultural Revolution as opponents of material incentives, bureaucratic control, and hierarchical privilege and as advocates of putting politics before economics in determining priorities and in allocating resources. Foreign observers labeled the contending sides "radicals" versus "moderates," but this nomenclature obscured the argument over ends and means which underlay the struggle for power.

These past surprises caution against long-range forecasting of the post-Mao leadership so far as particular personalities are concerned. Mao's absence further complicates prediction. His involvement in the political process from 1949 to 1976 was critical in determining the pattern and outcome of decision making. While his influence varied from one period to another, Mao's ability to legitimize or veto appointments and policies was unrivaled. It is not likely soon to be equaled by another individual. Yet the weight of Chinese tradition and political culture makes uncertain the stability of any leadership group that does not have a dominant central figure with the ultimate authority of an emperor or the Chairman.

Coincident with the death of this prime actor in China's political process is the culmination of developments that signal major changes in the makeup of party and government management. Like tectonic plates at work deep beneath the earth's surface, these slow, persistent, invisible movements suddenly break through the surface to change the faces that represent China to the world. One such force is simply the aging process. Death and transfiguration have already hit upper-level policy makers. The celebrated "Long March" veterans have largely left the scene. Their immediate subordinates, who became prominent in the 1950s, fell from grace during the Cultural Revolution of 1966-1968. Subsequent "rehabilitation" has often been more in name than authority.

In their place is a younger group of bureaucrats whose incremental rise to power was dramatically accelerated by the Cultural Revolution. Meanwhile, tension between older and younger officials, reflected in the official press, has complicated the policy process as it moves from higher levels of decision making to lower organs of implementation. In the next 10 years the original revolutionary generation will disappear entirely, leaving the system in the hands of those who entered political life after the founding of the PRC.

This passing of power from one generation to another raises questions of experience and perspective that must be left to speculation because so little is known of the people in line for higher party and governmental responsibility. Some change can be anticipated from those who have spent a lifetime in the bureaucracy rather than in fighting the Japanese invasion and the Chinese civil war. Other differences are likely to result from the provincial backgrounds of the newer officials in contrast to the more cosmopolitan careers of Chou En-lai's cohorts.

These two different sets of experiences can be interpreted as likely to have contradictory effects. Bureaucratic managers are more knowledgeable about economic and technical matters than are guerrilla fighters; in Western parlance, "they've had to meet a payroll." Yet these younger officials who rose through the system since 1949 have been largely isolated from the world (except those trained in the Soviet Union). In contrast, their Long March elders included many individuals with education and contacts abroad in Western Europe, Japan, and the United States. This exposure provided the older elite with a more sophisticated understanding of foreign societies than was attainable by their successors, particularly during the peak of China's isolation in the 1960s.

The typical bureaucratic newcomers to Peking have made their mark in mundane struggles with local production problems, mobilization campaigns, and consumer demand. Their priorities and perspectives differ from those of the centrally placed bureaucrats responsible for managing the world's most populous country and extending its influence in global matters. They may be more oriented toward domestic problems of economic development, stressing reliance on internal resources rather than on foreign imports that would enable the Chinese to match the industrial achievements of the more technologically advanced societies.

Changes in outlook and politics are also occurring within the PLA. Years of guerrilla warfare produced a well-defined elite that enjoyed considerable power in both Peking and the various regions under the separate responsibility of field armies. That elite won additional power when the chaos of Mao's Cultural Revolution required that martial law be imposed to guard against unruly Red Guards and urban disorder. However, Lin Piao's fall triggered a small but selective purge. Then in 1973 a reemergent civilian leadership asserted itself through the wholesale transfer of military commanders, depriving them of organizational bases that had been institutionalized through their continuous presence.

Meanwhile, modernization had brought new weaponry and capabilities, particularly air, naval, and nuclear. This development spawned different perspectives and interests as the traditional domination of ground forces eroded in the face of growing air and naval power. It also changed the relationship between the military and civilian sectors of the economy. The rising cost and increased complexity of modern weapons systems, conventional as well as nuclear, strained China's short supply of human and material resources. However, convergent interests were able to forge selective military-civilian coalitions in the struggle for budgetary allocations because research and development can serve more than one need. Thus the changing composition of the PLA has implications for patterns of decision making, organizational rivalry, and bureaucratic politics.

These shifting plates of political power that juxtapose differing generational, experiential, and vested interests caused increasingly overt tension from 1966 to 1976. Mao's effort to transform political conflict into constructive debate and development failed to produce a stable, well-ordered system that could resolve internal differences while maintaining a consistent external policy. For much of this decade, which constituted nearly one-third of the regime's life, repeated challenge from ideologically oriented anti-Establishment elements paralyzed or sharply modified policy on a wide range of domestic issues, initially in education and cultural affairs but ultimately impinging on economic matters as well.

Scattered evidence suggests that various components of the PLA took part in these disputes. During the Cultural Revolution, local ground commanders sided with conservative interests while air and naval units supported Red Guard elements in Peking. This split within the PLA stemmed from differing organizational perspectives rather than from opposing ideological convictions. The various field armies had been resident in their respective regions since 1949, but air and naval groups lacked any intimate and continuous association with particular localities and provincial leaders. In addition, China's ground forces depended mainly on infantry divisions with relatively little armored strength. This situation permitted them to rely largely on local resources. In contrast, the more technologically advanced air and naval forces required a strong and centralized administration to direct research and development as well as to supply sophisticated equipment produced by widely scattered industries.

These divergent interests within the military caution against extrapolating a simple dichotomy of military and civilian groups. An ideological faction may have no inherent appeal to the professionally oriented military officer, but if it can command the central government it may serve the need of those parts of the PLA dependent on that source and thereby win support. However, should that faction's policies jeopardize stability in the countryside that supplies most of the personnel and resources for 3.5 million ground troops, resistance from related PLA commands would be likely.

These divergent interests are also affected by foreign policy. The definition of military roles and missions ultimately deter-

19

mines resource allocation to provide necessary capabilities. More specifically, protection against a Soviet threat requires a strong ground and air defense but minimal naval support. However, combat contingencies that might involve Japan or the United States would place primary demand on air and naval strength. This definition of roles and missions, however, does not derive from a simple projection of enemy capabilities alone. In addition to estimates of enemy intentions, planners must take into account China's national interests and agree on how to rank priorities.

These logical inferences of how politics can influence military policy lack any direct evidence of how threat assessment, resource allocation, and military capabilities are actually determined in Peking. However, remarkably similar patterns of bureaucratic interaction have been found to persist in governments in other cultures, whether German, Japanese, or American. By analogy the Chinese bureaucracy, oldest in the world, is unlikely to be fundamentally different. Mao's personal primacy probably made "court politics" among individuals a distinguishing characteristic of his regime. But until a leader with similar overriding authority appears, Mao's successors will have to contend with coalitions vying to shape policy so that each receives a share of budgetary allocations.

These tensions can affect foreign policy, as they do regarding the interrelated issues of territorial integrity and ocean resources. These matters will be examined below in more detail, but a brief review of the central issues suffices at this point. From time to time, particularly since 1974, PRC propaganda has stressed the acquisition of "every inch of territory and every drop of water" claimed by China. In addition to their impact on the Sino-Soviet border dispute, these assertions have serious implications regarding the South China Sea, where scattered islands are contested by Hanoi, Manila, Taipei, and Peking. Moreover, of course, there is the question of the territorial integrity of Taiwan, northeast of which lie the unpopulated Senkakus, which are claimed by Taipei, Tokyo, and Peking. Finally, the problem of access to the continental shelf, with its potentially vast oil reserves stretching from the mainland to Korea, Japan, Taiwan, and the Philippines, is yet unresolved.

Responsibility for military support of China's interests in this
area falls primarily on its naval and air power, to which the army's
role is secondary. Thus, should politics in Peking be challenged
by xenophobic and nativistic factions that argue for unilateral
action to back China's claims, some elements of the PLA could
be mobilized on behalf of these factions and against those that
stress the importance of diplomatic and economic ties with
neighboring regimes.

With the post-Mao purge of Chiang Ch'ing and her three
Shanghai associates, the swing of the political pendulum would
seem to have stopped, signaling an apparent end to the debate that
had raged in one form or another since the inception of the
Cultural Revolution in early 1966. However, 10 years of purge
and rehabilitation, promotion and demotion, accusation and
counteraccusation have left a bitter legacy of personality and
policy differences that derive from real issues in domestic and
foreign policy. The choices are few and difficult. The fall of
Chiang Ch'ing marks a watershed in the seesaw struggle of suc-
cession but does not solve the problem of how China will preserve its revolutionary ethos while coping with modernization,
dependency, and "superpower hegemony." Continuous
appraisal of the political balance and trends of development is
necessary in order to forecast which mix of confrontation and
compromise is likely to characterize the PRC posture on
particular issues at any given time.

ECONOMIC FACTORS

Fortunately, forecasts concerning economic factors are
considerably easier than projections of the new leadership. There
is no prospect of China's becoming a global superpower or
alternatively of its facing utter collapse over the next decade.
Within these broad limits, however, estimates by outsiders range
between a future of modest incremental growth sufficient to meet
most of the essential needs of the population and one of recurring
crises resulting from intermittent natural disasters and political
mismanagement. The former view posits Chinese foreign policy

as relaxed and rationally determined by a combination of growing self-assurance and dependence on imports of foreign capital and technology, which will result in China's increased involvement in global affairs. This dependence is presently limited by a PRC refusal to accept credits of more than five years, but some observers believe the PRC may eventually seek longer-term loans, perhaps tied to future oil earnings. The less sanguine view stresses Peking's anxiety over foreign threats at times of domestic crisis. It suggests that this anxiety may combine with China's continuing priority on self-reliance to produce even greater tension and induce periodic withdrawal from foreign involvement.

Basic to all forecasts, however, is the continuing fragility of an economy that will soon encompass 1 billion persons, three-fourths of whom will be wholly dependent on agriculture. With only 15 percent of China's land arable, the pressure of population cannot be relieved by short-term palliatives. Nor is the long-term impact of birth control likely to bring relief in the 1980s. Extensive irrigation, electrification, mechanization, chemical fertilization, and multiple cropping will soon become exhausted as avenues of recourse for dramatic increases in yields. Despite efforts that have resulted in substantial increases in the amount of food produced, low caloric intake per capita remains approximately the same as that of 20 years ago. To be sure, famine has been avoided and more equitable distribution of food has made nutritional standards more equal throughout the countryside. Grain reserves can enable the population to subsist through crises that last one or two years, and annual imports help to feed coastal and northern cities. Nonetheless, the vulnerability of food supplies to climatic disruption and the inexorable demand of population increases is a constraint on Chinese power that is unlikely to be eliminated soon.

Less severe but no less important constraints exist in the shortage of capital for investment and imports and the shortage of material, human, and technological resources for modernizing industry. These problems are compounded to the extent that emphasis upon self-reliance excludes options such as joint venture agreements to introduce more foreign capital and technology. Moreover, the Cultural Revolution spawned an ethos that elevated "the masses" to equal status and authority with "experts." This ethos challenged the ability of trained specialists to make decisions and to direct complex and sophisticated economic programs. Few advanced research institutes have operated without interruption in the past 10 years, and almost no graduate programs are on a par with Soviet and Western counterparts. Thus China's ability to create and sustain its own technological advance will continue to be severely proscribed by the past cumulative damage, even if advanced training and basic research programs become more rationally directed and protected from interruption.

Meanwhile, accumulated savings and rising expectations fuel consumer demand at the same time that China's strategic force posture requires greater investment if a minimum deterrent capability is to be maintained against potential Soviet or American threats. Harsh authoritarian measures that attempt to force production increases without using meaningful material incentives and tangible rewards appear unfeasible in a country so large and populous as China. The growing political per-missiveness manifest during the past 10 years in wall posters and demonstrations, many of which articulate genuine economic grievances, may reflect recognition at high levels of the danger in simple suppression by bureaucratic or coercive methods. At the very least, this permissiveness has produced an atmosphere of limited but important freedom in communication that may prove difficult to reverse without jeopardizing political stability. Yet while expanding consumer demands confront the economy, the increasingly complex and costly modernization of industry and defense places competing demands on scarce human, material, and capital resources.

The dilemma is highlighted in the question of whether oil can be a solution to China's economic ills. According to United States government estimates, probable reserves will exceed projected domestic need for the balance of this century. However, whether oil is onshore or offshore, highly advanced technology is required for exploration, extraction, and refining. Foreign sources can supply this technology, but China will require large loans or major concessions if it is to tap these sources. Yet these steps seem precluded by self-imposed constraints rooted in the memory of "a century of shame and humiliation" engendered by foreign dependency and exploitation as well as a decade of "learning from the Soviet Union" that ended in open dispute and the sudden withdrawal of all Soviet experts in 1960.

In short, as more fully shown in Professor Dernberger's accompanying essay, whether one adopts a bullish or a bearish model of Chinese economic development, the limits of possible outcome fall within a relatively proscribed range. Though this reality will confront whatever leadership that may emerge with a relatively narrow set of alternatives with which to pursue foreign policy objectives, choices will remain nevertheless. Growing naval forces, manifest in a surface and submarine fleet sufficient to challenge immediate neighbors in the East China and South China seas, can extend PLA power beyond the continent. A modest but significant military assistance capacity can provide selected weaponry to nearby North Korea or the distant United Arab Republic. Military training, small arms, and funds can be given to insurgents throughout the Third World. Economic aid can build roads in Nepal or railroads in Africa. China will, of necessity, "not become a superpower," just as its leaders proclaim. It will, however, be a middle-range power capable of affecting its immediate environment and influencing selected developments in other regions.

ISSUES AND OPTIONS

The issues facing the Peking leadership over the next decade resemble to an amazing degree those that have confronted successive Chinese regimes throughout the past century: security, territorial integrity, economic development, and dependency on foreign powers. These issues are inextricably interrelated; moreover, they are inherent in China's vast size and backward condition. Solutions are neither obvious nor simple, and debate over both piecemeal and overall approaches has wracked politics and policy in Peking. Gradually, however, the worst threats to security as perceived by Peking have diminished

24

and, except for Taiwan, territorial integrity is nearly complete. Although the economy is at a "safe" stage of self-sufficiency, the pace and direction of development in the coming decade will pose critical problems that relate directly to the issue of foreign dependency.

In the vital area of national security, China is no longer in danger of being nibbled away, as it was during the Ch'ing dynasty, or of being invaded by Japan, as it was in the first half of this century. The threat of American support for landings by Chinese Nationalist forces from Taiwan peaked in the 1950s, but disappeared with the Shanghai Communiqué concluded at the end of President Nixon's visit to China in February 1972. Fear of a Soviet invasion remained high from 1968 to the mid-1970s, but gradually ebbed as PLA nuclear capability expanded and posed a deterrent threat to Soviet cities. While China's pledge of no-first-use for nuclear weapons removed them as a deterrent against conventional attack, they have increased in number to provide greater reassurance against a Soviet nuclear strike.

Nevertheless, security considerations retain high priority in Peking. The vastly superior Soviet power can never be wholly disregarded, particularly as a potential force for intervention in a prolonged political crisis such as that which occurred in Czechoslovakia in 1968. So long as more than 750,000 troops, backed by powerful rocket and air power, remain around China's northern and western borders, "worst case" scenarios must be included in preparations for any contingency. Should India, Japan, or the United States substitute a threatening array of military force for their present postures, additional security concerns will arise.

One way China's leaders could defuse these concerns would be to reduce Sino-Soviet confrontation. A border settlement, provided it was accompanied by mutual withdrawal of forces and a political détente, could relieve both sides of costly military deployments along the 4,500-mile frontier. The area in actual dispute is minimal in both size and strategic significance, except for a disputed island opposite Khabarovsk at the confluence of the Amur and Ussuri rivers. Détente between Peking and Moscow is a distinct possibility now that Mao is gone. Mao's opponents have been accused, by implication, of disagreeing with his intransigence in the Sino-Soviet dispute. Meanwhile, China specialists in Moscow have frankly expressed hope of improved relations after his demise. The depth and extent of bitterness on both sides has been compounded by the many manifestations of the dispute, which has been waged on a global basis both in open forums and in covert competition. Nevertheless, the dispute's immediate impact on national security suggests a need for the reduction of tension in direct, bilateral confrontation.

During the next decade, political considerations are likely to reinforce security concerns in leading toward reductions in the level of Sino-Soviet conflict. Both Peking and Moscow realize how Washington exploited their confrontation by playing off one side against the other after the 1971 Kissinger trip to Peking. The PRC in particular could improve its bargaining position by maintaining a more proximate balance between the two superpowers. China's ideological opposition to "imperialism" pits its policy against American interests in Korea and Southeast Asia even while the common opposition of Peking and Washington to Soviet influence produces parallel policies elsewhere. Moreover, so long as Taiwan remains an issue in Sino-American relations, the advantages of détente with Moscow carry potential political weight in Peking. While some Chinese leaders might warn that an accommodation with the Soviets would strain ties with Washington and further decrease the likelihood of agreement on Taiwan, others might discount such agreement as not forthcoming in any case or argue that movement toward Moscow is the only way of influencing Washington to look more favorably upon the PRC's demands. Finally, the fluctuating nature of Soviet-American relations and the relative balance of power between the superpowers may give additional impetus for China to maintain equidistance in its dealings with both sides.

Territorial integrity has posed two kinds of problems for Chinese rulers over the past century. One problem has concerned the common need to define borders and to defend border regions against invasion and annexation. In the event of defeat, irredentist sentiment could pose demands for the recovery of "lost territory." The second problem, foreign penetration, while not unique to China, has emerged as almost equally important. It arose from the fact that the borderlands most distant from central rule are predominantly inhabited by non-Chinese peoples. Although they comprise less than 5 percent of the total population, the Mongols, Kazakhs, Uighurs, Tibetans, and other ethnic minorities distributed along a vast periphery that is separated from China proper by mountains and deserts have provided tempting bait for foreign subversion. The possibility of subversion proved particularly threatening whenever the central regime was weakened by internal disunity or economic crisis.

Since 1949 border delimitation has been negotiated with all China's neighbors except India and the Soviet Union. Roads, railroads, and airfields have extended military power to the out-lying regions. This power was dramatically demonstrated in the brief Sino-Indian War of 1962. Taiwan poses the only major outstanding territorial issue. By comparison, the minuscule islands and reefs in dispute, such as the Spratleys in the South China Sea and the Senkakus between Taiwan and Okinawa, have little relevance to the question of territorial integrity per se. Their significance relates basically to ocean resources, primarily oil, where possession provides access; their symbolic importance as a political claim is only secondary.

Considerable uncertainty remains concerning Taiwan. Prior to World War II, Mao Tse-tung conceded the possibility that Taiwan might remain independent after the expulsion of Japanese colonial rule. However, the wartime Cairo and Potsdam agreements promised to return all territory seized from China by Japan, whereupon Mao's position naturally changed. Since 1949 every major statement from Peking has pledged the "liberation of Taiwan" as an ultimate goal. When and how this would occur remained a subject of dispute between Chinese and Americans throughout the initial ambassadorial negotiations between 1955 and 1958 as well as after the Nixon trip of 1972.

If the politics of Peking continue to make Taiwan an irreconcilable issue of territorial integrity, then a major dilemma will confront the leadership. It is unlikely that influential groups in Taiwan will voluntarily accept communist rule. The extreme disparity of living standards and life-styles makes the island more attractive than the mainland to them. Therefore union, if it is to be achieved, must be forcibly imposed. Yet Taiwan's distance and defenses make invasion a formidable task. Moreover, China's relations with Japan, its major economic partner, would be significantly disrupted by the use of force against Taiwan, where Japanese economic and emotional ties are second only to those of the United States. The consequences could cause a major effort by Japan to strengthen its military forces, perhaps including the acquisition of nuclear weapons. Needless to say, the impact on Sino-American relations would be far more severe.

Compulsive irredentism is not characteristic of Chinese behavior despite the contrary tone of Peking's propaganda. PRC border agreements with Mongolia, Afghanistan, Nepal, and Burma have involved compromise of past claims. The de facto border with India concedes the large eastern sector, formerly known as the Northeast Frontier Agency, in exchange for a larger unpopulated region in the western Himalayan heights. This concession is noteworthy because it was the eastern sector that Chinese troops overran during the 1962 war, after which Peking announced a unilateral cease-fire and withdrawal from all territory that had recently been occupied. These precedents raise the possibility that Taiwan may eventually lose its status as an issue of territorial integrity. This depends, however, on politics in Peking, the eventual identity of the island, and the international implications of a decision by Peking to acquiesce in the status quo rather than attempt to seize Taiwan by force.

Beginning in 1950, the United States intervened in the Chinese civil war to safeguard Taiwan from communist take-over. It provided $2.5 billion in military assistance to arm Nationalist troops, placed nuclear-capable missiles on the island, and built military bases that supported air attacks against North Vietnam. However, the Sino-American communiqué of February 1972 pledged the "ultimate" withdrawal of all United States military forces as a step toward the establishment of full diplomatic relations between Peking and Washington. Implicit was the Chinese expectation that the 1954 Mutual Assistance Treaty concluded between Taipei and Washington would expire at some point in the near future. The White House, however, constrained by ensuing events—Watergate, Indochina, and a preelection challenge from the Republican right—strengthened Taiwan's military defenses and left the security agreement intact.

While it is quite likely that this Gordian knot will be cut by 1980, enough past predictions have proven misfounded to caution against this one as well. The issue could become a political football in Peking. In an unstable leadership situation, there is a temptation to exploit an opponent's political weakness, particularly over a nationalistic issue such as Taiwan. Such a situation could arise over the leadership's failure to progress visibly toward terminating the United States military guarantee or its softness in negotiating an agreement, implied or expressed, not to use force in "the liberation of Taiwan." In the absence of an authoritative figure such as Mao or Chou, coalitional confrontation could deadlock discussions. On the one side would be advocates of an unyielding nationalistic posture, militant ideological opponents of "United States imperialism," and vested military interests in the navy and air forces. On the other side would be foreign affairs specialists who advocate balancing superpower relations, and foreign trade proponents who team with domestic planners to argue that China's development and economic modernization depend on Japanese and American technology. In view of the subtlety and sensitivity of a formula on Taiwan's future that would be mutually acceptable in Peking and Washington, this confrontation might prevent a viable solution.

This analysis highlights the interrelationship of several issues: national security, territorial integrity, economic development, and foreign dependency. Before we examine the latter two problems in more detail, one final aspect of the Taiwan problem, namely, the offshore islands of Quemoy and Matsu, deserves attention. Located within 3 and 10 miles, respectively, of the mainland, these Chinese Nationalist outposts contain nearly 100,000 Taiwanese troops. The PLA tried to invade Quemoy in 1949 and failed. It attempted blockade and bombardment in 1958 and failed. Since then few serious shellings and no major military action have occurred.

Nevertheless an optional strategy exists for Peking whereby a total blockade without bombardment would isolate the islands from Taiwan. This blockade could then be exploited for blackmail leverage on the families and relatives of the beleaguered troops to pressure the Nationalist authorities into negotiations with the PRC. The United States has no commitment to defend Quemoy and Matsu. A 1955 congressional resolution that enabled President Eisenhower to aid the Nationalists in 1958 was nullified by Congress in 1975. Thus advocates of a more aggressive approach can apply pressure on the offshore islands as a low-risk alternative to targeting the main island of Taiwan itself.

The prospects for a successful use of force against Taiwan are remote but cannot be wholly excluded. The PRC lacks sufficient amphibious and airborne transportation to support an invasion across the 100 miles of water separating Taiwan from the mainland in the strength necessary to overwhelm the island's more than 400,000 troops. Prolonged bombardment or nuclear attack would destroy Taiwan's flourishing economy, which makes the island so valuable a prize for Peking. A naval blockade would probably fail unless major changes were to occur in the respective air and naval forces of the two sides. Moreover, while such a move would be legal so long as the civil war remained in force, should Taiwan eventually declare itself a new independent state the blockade would then constitute interference with freedom of the seas and arouse considerable reaction abroad. Finally, Peking could attempt to isolate Taiwan by threatening its various trading partners with economic sanctions should they continue to provide resources and markets. The success of this, however, would depend on how much each country relied on China for exports or imports.

Compared with territorial integrity, problems of economic development and foreign dependency are less dramatic but no less volatile issues of debate. Modernization and industrial growth are necessary if China is to meet the domestic needs of its future 1 billion inhabitants and the potential threats posed by the Soviet Union, Japan, and the United States. Yet the pace and direction of economic development will be severely proscribed unless China imports substantial amounts of foreign technology that in turn would require large exports in order to earn foreign exchange.

Nineteenth-century conservatives opposed opening China to the world, warning that this would destroy the Confucian tradition. Their opponents in favor of "modernization" argued that if China was to be strong enough to safeguard its sovereignty and independence, policy must seek to introduce Western methods while preserving the essence of Chinese civilization. Similar debates have recurred over the past 30 years. Initially concern arose over reliance on the Soviet Union for economic development. More recently the importation of whole plants and advanced technology from Japan, the United States, and Western Europe has caused fresh controversy. Opponents of a "slavish mentality toward foreign things" have championed "self-reliance." Their position was more persuasive in 1974, when inflation drove prices of imports up while recession sent prices of exports down. That year the PRC balance of payments showed a $1 billion deficit.

Nevertheless, in January 1975 Premier Chou En-lai announced that by the year 2000 China would catch up with the advanced nations of the world in industry, science, technology, and defense. His cohorts in these various sectors recognized that China's indigenous human and material resources alone could not "bootstrap" such growth. They also recognized the hazards of dependency—namely, that it would provide potential leverage to foreign states, including former enemies such as Japan and the United States. They therefore refused long-term loans and joint projects. In the final analysis, however, they insisted not only that the risks were worth the gains but also that they must be accepted if China were to maintain full independence and achieve genuine security in the long term.

With Chou's death the debate broke out anew. Teng's fall immediately thereafter was accompanied by a revival of the argument previously voiced in 1974 prior to Chou's authoritative pronouncement. By mid-1976 negotiations for whole-plant technology had ground to a halt as foreign business representatives sensed confusion and caution in their Chinese

31

counterparts concerning the pace, direction, and composition of technological imports and raw materials exports. Then the ouster of Chiang Ch'ing and her three Shanghai associates in the aftermath of Mao's death was followed by fresh reassurances that China's foreign trade would pursue the line established by Chou.

Although the debate seemed ended for the present, it could recur in the future with far-reaching implications for China's international relations during the remainder of this century. Access to and reliance upon foreign technology will determine the capability of PRC military power to reach from the continent to targets in the Soviet Union, India, and the United States, whether by land- or sea-launched missiles. It will also define the PRC defensive capability against attack by ground or air forces. As standardization and automation spread throughout the world, China's willingness to import technology will determine its dependency on close and continuing economic relations abroad. It will also delineate particular bilateral ties, whether Sino-Japanese or Sino-American, as of greater or lesser economic importance, thereby shaping political relationships.

More fundamentally, the outcome of this debate will also influence domestic developments. The common concern of Confucian and communist conservatives over the impact of foreign penetration is merited. Technology and whole plants transcend their physical equipment and presence in their effect on human relationships and social values. The changing role of technical experts and the rewards for expertise, the hierarchical structure of complex organization, and the need for centralized direction of intimately interrelated production inputs are but a few of the areas in which the modernization process is likely to have social implications.

Probably the most dramatic revelation of mutually opposed alternatives in foreign policy posture broke to the surface during the Cultural Revolution. In May 1967 a militant faction within the foreign ministry led youthful Red Guard gangs in a seizure of the offices, ransacking its files and throwing them out the window. In August a mob burned the British chancellery and shouted revolutionary rhetoric throughout the diplomatic colony via loudspeakers and endless demonstrations. Chinese embassies abroad echoed these sentiments, as all ambassadors save one were recalled for examination and indoctrination. Active support and encouragement in circles adjacent to Mao, including his wife, Chiang Ch'ing, showed the Chinese turmoil to be more than the youthful excesses concurrently manifest in the Western world.

Against this xenophobic defiance of diplomatic relations and economic dependency stood the targets of Red Guard wrath. Chou En-lai, besieged in his office for two days, stood his ground and subsequently apologized to those foreign leaders and governments—other than Moscow—with whom relations had been most seriously impaired. His minister of foreign affairs, Ch'en I, vigorously denied the radicals' accusations that he had betrayed the revolution. Ch'en also warned against the risks of militancy in foreign relations. Many figures prominent in international political and economic negotiations disappeared for several years or suffered public vilification in wall poster and newspaper attacks but later reappeared in their previous positions.

In short, a violent anti-Establishment assault combined nativistic, chauvinistic, xenophobic, and revolutionary impulses to force a policy of militant confrontation on China. In its denial of accepted international norms, this policy fundamentally meant withdrawal from foreign affairs, although ostensibly it called for greater engagement on the international revolutionary front. In opposition stood the Establishment, convinced that China's weakness and vulnerability coupled with its potential international role required caution and compromise in order to attain a position of maximum participation and influence in world affairs.

The crisis was short-lived. The peak disruption of foreign relations lasted only from May to September 1967. However, the consequences of disruption, internal and external, extended well into 1970–1971. The combination of Mao's belief that "contradictions" are inherent in all situations and his determination to handle them as "nonantagonistic"—subject to creative manipulation and constructive development—caused

33

him to play a crucial role in these developments, straddling both sides of the debate. In the process, however, misjudgment and mismanagement badly damaged China's image abroad.

More than China's image was at stake in the behavior of militant Red Guards on the Hong Kong border and the Sino-Soviet frontier. From May to September 1967 the British colony endured weeks of strikes, mass demonstrations, and small-scale terrorist bombings without serious threat to internal security. However, in July unidentifiable automatic weapons fire opened up from both sides of the border on a police post, killing and wounding its occupants. Hong Kong's minuscule defense force faced a risk of escalation that potentially involved the PLA. Fortunately the attack ceased when Ghurka troops moved into the area, but lesser crises arose as recurring violence threatened border security. Finally, the PLA quietly came to Hong Kong's rescue. It established special checkpoints to detain or shoot militants from Canton who pledged to "liberate our oppressed compatriots from British fascism," and it secretly negotiated with Hong Kong authorities for joint suppression of illegal activities near the border.

We know little about similar incidents on the Sino-Soviet frontier, but later accounts and accusations exchanged by both sides indicate that belligerent Red Guard provocations occurred there as well. These would have confirmed Soviet concern over possible Chinese intentions to recover "lost territory" in Siberia and the Maritime Provinces, aggressively asserted by Mao in 1964 through an interview with visiting Japanese socialists. Moscow's reaction was to increase its military strength throughout the 4,500-mile frontier area, thereby heightening Chinese concern over Soviet intent. In 1969 the mutually perceived hostility and resulting tensions exploded in larger border clashes that threatened to involve both nations in major conflict.

Mao's death removes the major point of support for advocates of militancy in China's foreign relations. The fall of Chiang Ch'ing and her associates underscores this point. Considerations of China's weakness and the long-run need for economic growth based on imports of foreign technology will determine a pattern of foreign policy based on caution and compromise rather than confrontation.

Short-run deviation from this pattern is possible nevertheless. Should the leadership be divided and subject to internal challenge between contending factions, postures of intransigence and belligerency may emerge in foreign affairs. Regardless of whether they represent a temporary ascendance by a militant coalition or a protective reaction by a more moderate group that feels vulnerable to attack, these postures must be taken into account by other governments whose immediate interests are involved. The events of 1967 demonstrate the need to avoid an overreaction that might lock Chinese behavior into a more rigid posture than otherwise might develop. It also suggests the interplay between the behavior of other states and domestic politics in China. To a limited degree, the strength of contending factions may depend on the credibility of their respective positions concerning foreign policy, which in turn rests on how other governments interact with China.

TWO

The Chinese Vision of World Affairs

It is difficult to delineate a single Chinese world view that is uniformly held throughout the society or even within the elite that formulates policy. Not only is direct contact with Chinese limited for foreigners, but determining whether the inner image held by high officials is identical with that offered verbally is virtually impossible. Nonetheless, there is sufficient consistency and coherence in the articulation of a general, overarching perspective to warrant at least a summary sketch of its main components.

THE IDEOLOGICAL COMPONENT

Chinese perceptions and expections are shaped by an ideological framework that is articulated daily through aural and visual media from the break of sunrise to the hour of retirement at night. This constant flow of indoctrination intermittently contains modifications and new formulations, but the basic ingredients remain the same amalgam of Marx, Lenin, and Mao. Changes of PRC posture in foreign affairs are explained in theoretical terms describing the "principal contradictions of the present era." Often these explanations initially emerge in programmatic statements on the occasion of a major political meeting or an annual celebration, such as New Year's Day or National Day. The key concepts subsequently reappear ritualistically in editorials, speeches inside China and elsewhere, and joint communiqués signed with visiting dignitaries.

Foreign audiences and analysts may find their senses dulled by the rhetoric and repetitiveness of Peking's verbiage, but it would be wrong to dismiss its impact on those who decide and effect policy. Ideology is the basic reference point from which the Chinese understand world affairs, set policy goals, and define the legitimate means of pursuing these goals. It provides the lenses that shape the view of events, defining certain phenomena as relevant and setting the analytical framework for interpreting them. This is not to suggest that PRC policy makers are unique in their orientation. Most social systems have some such cognitive cohesion, and no nation-state is without it. What distinguishes the Chinese vision from others, including its Soviet counterpart, is the degree of consciousness, uniformity, and apparent commitment with which ideology is reflected in the foreign policy process.

This study will examine the practical component of policy below, but the gap between theory and practice is worth noting at the outset lest its emphasis be misunderstood. In addition, it must be recognized that as a triumphant revolutionary movement, Chinese communism has so far experienced only one generation of leadership and that under the direction of its prime ideologist. How Mao's passing and the rise of a new generation of leaders will affect the situation a decade hence can only be surmised. Comparison with similar movements suggests that the intensity of belief will diminish as the responsibility of meeting the daily needs of society becomes more prominent. However, a brief review of the function and content of the ideological component in Chinese society puts this assertion in question.

Initially, the new regime undertook an intensive "reeducation" of the populace to counter foreign influences that had been accumulated over "a century of shame and humiliation." These influences were transmitted through personal and institutional contacts and resulted in the aforementioned "slavish mentality toward foreign things." Almost all industrial products, for instance, even nails and matches, were imported. If China was to "stand up" in action it would first have to do so in spirit, according to Mao. Hence a reshaping of the national vision was in order.

The obverse of this "inferiority complex" was Sinocentrism, or "great Han chauvinism," that viewed the outer world—traditionally "barbarian"—with contempt or indifference. This attitude was equally anathema to Mao, who sought to involve China in world affairs as a genuinely revolutionary power with equal concern for and help to all "oppressed peoples" regardless of status, development, or race. His vision required a basic reorientation of China's perspective toward former tributary states such as Korea, Vietnam, and Burma as well as remote African colonies wholly beyond the ken of imperial China.

In addition to these ideological imperatives, Mao believed that China's foreign relations should become part of daily life through slogans, propaganda campaigns, and mass demonstrations. The first decade of PRC rule was one of total dependence on the Soviet Union for military and economic development; support for Sino-Soviet friendship saturated the media. But in the next 10 years Sino-Soviet polemics led to bloody border clashes. Chinese domestic propaganda reversed gears with an intensity equal to that of the "learn from the Soviet Union" period. Similarly, from 1949 to 1970 "United States imperialism" dominated the media as a menace to the world in general and China in particular. Suddenly the line changed with Kissinger's visit in 1971 and Mao's reception of Nixon in 1972, whereupon Mao's "united front" exhortations of the anti-Japanese war were revived to justify attacking "the main enemy" by joining with "all who can be united in opposition." Thereafter "social imperialism" consistently was the target of harsher and more detailed diatribes than "United States imperialism."

Thus, whether in China's defiant isolation or in its speeches to world councils and United Nations assemblages on such issues as population, food, and law of the sea, the larger ideological framework has been and still is invoked to explain the pertinence of particular developments for all levels of society. Consequently, a rapid spread of awareness and information about other countries has transformed the consciousness of the populace. *People's Daily* devotes a percentage of space to foreign affairs higher than that of any other mass newspaper in the world. Its editorials and dispatches are reprinted in provincial papers and disseminated over the loudspeaker system that fills factories, farms, schools, and streets with an endless flow of indoctrination. Chinese who have grown up in the last 30 years necessarily see the world and its various components through a Marxist-Maoist prism. Mao's death will not alter this vision for some time. Indeed the new generation of leaders may find it more acceptable than other visions for policy making, since they developed in the totally controlled and isolated environment of 1949–1970, whereas the elite of Liu Shao-ch'i, Chou En-lai, and Teng Hsiao-p'ing were more cosmopolitan.

The resulting perspectives are familiar enough not to require extensive elaboration here. A simple recapitulation is in order, however, as a reminder of the differences between Chinese visions and more or less sophisticated communist variants elsewhere. One of the Chairman's widely quoted phrases offers a pithy summation of the explicitly anti–status quo nature of his ideology: "The current international situation is excellent; there is great disorder under heaven." The two-part proposition is a harmonic whole. No "but" separates opposite thrusts as in another of Mao's publicized statements: "The danger of a new world war still exists and the people of all countries must get prepared. But revolution is the main trend in the world today." War is undesirable yet possible; revolution is both desired and likely.

Marxist assumptions of class conflict, Leninist strictures against "imperialism, the highest stage of capitalism," and Maoist attacks on "Soviet revisionism" set the basic framework of analysis. Within this framework the periodic categorization of nations distinguishes gradations of good and bad, friend and foe. In 1954 the rigid "two-camp" Soviet view was changed by Peking to four groupings: the socialist "camp," the United States, America's reluctant allies and former enemies, and newly emergent states. China's diplomatic offensive in the Afro-Asian world followed thereafter. Ten years later, this fourfold formulation was revived to herald the winning of diplomatic recognition from France and to acknowledge reliance on Western Europe for the importation of whole plants and technology. More recently Chinese statements have focused on the "superpowers," the "Second World" of advanced industrial states, and the "Third World" of less developed countries (which includes the PRC itself).

These categories are further subdivided, depending on the occasion to which they refer, into "the main enemy" and "the lesser enemy" or "the people" and "the oppressors." The "main enemy" necessarily changes from one time to another, varying among "United States imperialism," "Japanese militarism," and "Soviet social imperialism." Mao's celebrated civil war formulation is applied equally to foreign policy: "Use contradiction, obtain majority, oppose minority, destroy each group, develop the progressive force, win over the middle roaders, isolate stubborn elements, be reasonable, and be calculating."

This detailed formulation is often subsumed under the united front strategy, which has two variants derived from Lenin. The variant "from above" links ruling groups—including feudal sheikdoms, despotic monarchies, and military dictatorships—in common cause against such enemies as "militant Zionism" or "superpower hegemony." Alternatively, the "united front from below" joins intellectuals, national capitalists, petty bourgeoisie, workers, peasants, and dissident military elements against these same ruling groups. Thus, today's ally may be tomorrow's enemy.

The second variant is sometimes pursued simultaneously with the first. Burma's Prime Minister, Ne Win, has been ceremoniously received in Peking while the Burmese Communist Party was being praised for its "armed struggle" against Rangoon's troops. Chinese officials explain this dichotomy as a function of the difference between state-to-state and party-to-party relations. The interlocking of party and state through both dual membership of key persons and the decision-making process itself makes a mockery of this distinction. Nevertheless, it persists as a formal justification for the two-pronged policy.

Speaking at the height of Cultural Revolution radicalism in 1967, Mao privately defined China's role in blunt terms: "We—China—are not only the political center of world revolution but moreover in military matters and technology must also become the center of world revolution. . . . We must become the arsenal of world revolution." This paraphrase of President Franklin D. Roosevelt's call during World War II for America to become "the arsenal of democracy" has so far had far less consequence than its 1940 antecedent. Nevertheless, it reveals a basic ideological thrust of potential importance.

The Sinocentrism of Mao's statement together with the dynamism and disruption in the Marxist-Maoist world vision present a formidable challenge to advocates in other nations of Chinese participation in global planning for orderly, managed change and compromise solutions to outstanding problems. At the extreme, the xenophobic Red Guard violence of 1967 recalled the Boxers of 1900. More recently, assertive attacks on "both superpowers" in support of Third World demands echo the more strident call for "armed struggle against imperialism and colonialism" that was issued immediately after the founding of the regime in 1949. Neither angry withdrawal nor aggressive involvement in world affairs is currently a dominant impulse in China, but they remain potential deviations from the main course of policy. Whether they resurface in the future may well be determined by the nonideological, or "practical," component in policy.

THE PRACTICAL COMPONENT

Mao's writings constantly admonish his followers to merge theory with practice. He explicitly inveighs against dogmatism, or blind adherence to theory in defiance of reality, and argues that theory must be revised according to experience. These admonitions are reflected in conversations with Chinese officials who acknowledge the difference between principle and practice. While this difference is commonplace in politics, both communist and noncommunist, the conscious explication of such contradictions is unique to the Chinese leadership. The belief that theory should be revised according to experience justifies an impressive degree of flexibility within a fairly rigid ideological framework. Policy shifts that may appear to other nations as stemming from sheer opportunism are interpreted by Peking through major statements, editorials, and instructional commentaries as in fact lying directly within this theoretical context.

An additional discrepancy, of course, exists between public propaganda and private perception. Even in the mid-1950s, Mao secretly denied that there was danger of an attack from the United States against China or the Soviet Union and denigrated American military strength as posing no serious threat. Reassuring his audience, Mao specifically warned, "We must not be misled by our propaganda." Similarly, in 1971 Chou En-lai responded to James Reston's query concerning the vehemence of anti-Japanese statements by saying, "You just heard some of our slogans."

Examples abound of the degree to which reality overrules rhetoric and practical considerations prevail over theoretical. Mao long ago publicly described the United States as "a paper tiger"; during his first decade of rule mass campaigns periodically vowed to "liberate Taiwan." Yet, in 1959 Mao privately explained why the PLA had been able to crush a revolt in Tibet but unable to take Taiwan: "Tibet has no other country that has signed a treaty with it like Taiwan. Our air force can go there, also our army. Now the Taiwan situation is entirely different. Taiwan signed a treaty with America."[1] In sum, China's military inferiority was a decisive constraint when its attempt to secure national unity and territorial integrity was faced with United States power. As Mao conceded another time in answering an unidentified questioner: "Since it [United States imperialism] is a

[1] "Speech to the 16th Supreme State Conference," April 15, 1959, in *Mao Tse-tung, ssu-hsiang wan sui!* [Long Live the Thought of Mao Tse-tung], a collection of Mao's speeches, memoranda, and remarks from 1955 to 1967 (1969 edition), p. 289. This collection, distributed from Taiwan, was published clandestinely on the mainland. It is available in most universities where there are centers of Chinese studies.

paper tiger, why do we not attack Taiwan?. . . It is both a real and a paper tiger. Temporarily it appears as real; in the long run it can be seen to be paper."[2]

During that "long run," however, practical considerations imposed a further constraint on policy. From 1949 to 1969 Peking stridently denounced the United States as the main evil in the world. Then, suddenly faced with a perceived threat of attack from the Soviet Union, Mao signaled an interest in détente with the United States and in February 1972 publicly shook President Nixon's hand while American bombers pounded communist forces in adjacent Indochina. The "paper tiger" became a tacit ally in the face of a threat from the "polar bear" to the north.

Sino-American relations demonstrate China's professed insistence on principle and the compromise of principle in practice. For more than 15 years PRC statements demanded that the United States must withdraw from Taiwan and the Taiwan Strait before any relations could be established. The Shanghai Communiqué contained only an ambiguous American agreement not to "challenge" assertions that Taiwan was part of China, together with a pledge for the "ultimate withdrawal" of all United States military forces and bases; yet these American "concessions" sufficed to being a limited détente.

In December 1972 Chinese officials continued to tell American visitors that because of the "two-China" problem there could be no PRC presence in Washington so long as the Chinese Nationalists remained there. Then in February 1973 Chou En-lai agreed that "liaison offices" should be established in both capitals, thereby tacitly accepting the diplomatic presence of the Republic of China. Perhaps Chou's concern over his health after the discovery of his cancer in 1972 persuaded Peking to establish permanent, professional channels of communication in lieu of the intermittent personal visits by Kissinger that had characterized the Sino-American relationship until then. Whatever the reason, the result was a major compromise in Peking's principled opposition to "two Chinas."

[2]"Speech with Heads of Cooperatives," November 30, 1958, in *Mao Tse-tung, ssu-hsiang wan sui!*, p. 255.

PRC entry into the United Nations aroused widespread fear that Peking's embitterment over exclusion from 1949 to 1971 and its revolutionary impulses would confront the Security Council with repeated vetoes and deliberate obstructionism. How, in this public forum under world scrutiny, could Peking's diplomats avoid taking action that would support their avowed principles? Taking a cue from precedent, the Chinese representatives quietly encouraged the expanded use of a consensual approach whereby all discussion occurs informally before general agreement emerges through a draft resolution or a presidential statement, with or without a vote. Frequently Peking's delegate chose "nonparticipation," which could be interpreted as passive opposition in accordance with principle or as a means of tacit cooperation. These two PRC tactics facilitated passage of more than two-thirds of the resolutions adopted during the first four years of its participation in the United Nations.[3] The veto will not be unilaterally renounced by China despite its obvious connotations of inequality for nonpermanent Council members. But neither will China abuse the veto power in rigid support of principle at the risk of alienating potential United Nations support and perhaps completely hamstringing the organization.

THEORY VERSUS PRACTICE

The fact that principle is often compromised in practice neither resolves the underlying tension nor precludes reversals of priority between the two poles of policy decisions. Dramatic shifts back and forth have prompted speculation about possible cyclical causes, such as the alternating ascendancy of rival factions.

Mao personally exemplified the tension and fluctuations in his handling of Sino-Soviet relations. In 1949–1950 he deferred to Stalin's demands for concessions in northeast China and joint stock companies in order to secure a defense commitment and modest economic assistance. In 1959–1960, Mao challenged

[3] This analysis is based on an unpublished paper by Professor Samuel S. Kim of Monmouth College, presented at a workshop on Chinese foreign policy at the University of Michigan in Ann Arbor, summer 1976.

Khruschev on ideological and political grounds in order to protect China's socioeconomic development from the corrosion of communist values that he saw as embodied in the Soviet stress on material incentives, hierarchical relationships, and technological imperatives, as transmitted through Soviet advice. His compromise with Stalin laid the foundations for military and economic development. His refusal to compromise with Khrushchev slowed development and imposed new defense burdens of considerable cost.

Mao's final years were devoted to ensuring that the "contradiction," or tension, between theory and practice would continue after his death. This contradiction was evident in Mao's two closest associates, Chou En-lai and Chiang Ch'ing, who, respectively, symbolized the practical and ideological. More broadly, developments after 1971 fostered two categories of consciousness concerning foreign affairs. On the one hand, thousands of Chinese became increasingly exposed to and involved in the outside world through the burgeoning PRC participation in international organizations, conferences, and trade as well as in scientific and technological exchanges both abroad and within China. This exposure and involvement introduced a flood of information and yielded experience that affected the perceptions of the individuals involved and ultimately the organizations with which they are affiliated. On the other hand, repeated attacks in the press and wall posters aroused various groups, students and workers in particular, against those figures who seemed most likely to increase China's accommodation with the existing international system. Campaigns of a thinly veiled allegorical nature triggered widespread debate over many issues. Although these issues were primarily domestic in nature, their implications for foreign trade and dependency were far-reaching. At the same time, films, plays, and pamphlets attempted to perpetuate painful memories of the Japanese invasion and the American fighting in Korea, despite significantly improved relations with both Japan and the United States.

These two developments juxtapose a cosmopolitan, sophisticated view against a primitive, purist sense of the world.

Moreover, even those persons with superb linguistic and diplomatic skills who have been exposed to foreign lands and peoples often share with their untraveled associates a residual bitterness against China's past treatment, a keen sense of slight from implied inequality, and a genuine resentment against Soviet and American exploitation of superpower status. Thus, depending upon domestic political pressures and the behavior of foreign governments, persons who might otherwise argue for compromise and against confrontation could be moved, contrary to their practical judgment, to defer to ideological exponents of policy.

The implications of these alternative postures for specific issues will be examined in the following section. However, the earlier forecast bears repeating as a general projection for the next decade: the factions favoring accommodation and negotiation are likely to prevail over those supporting unilateral action and the use of force. This likelihood may be obscured by aggressive verbal posturing and the temporary ascendancy of ideological imperatives, but practical considerations will continue to dominate China's overall behavior.

China's military vulnerability to superpower attack will preclude adventuristic forays that invite Soviet or American retaliation. Major Chinese military ventures are unlikely in the next decade, regardless of domestic politics, because of the practical constraints of military power. China's continuing dependence on food imports is an additional constraint on actions that would risk an embargo from important sources of grain, such as Canada and the United States. Uncertain weather and a population growth rate that is barely surpassed by increases in harvests make the possibility of an embargo a serious consideration for Peking, at least until the middle of the next decade.

China's dependence on imports of foreign technology is a less serious constraint in the short run, although it could become critical should such sources again be cut off for many years. This threat would pertain particularly to Sino-Japanese trade, which comprises more than one-fourth of total PRC foreign commerce, including imports of essential iron and steel, whole plants, machine tools, and chemical fertilizers. Since the effects of disruption are not as immediate or vital in the case of technology as they are with food imports, a prolonged debate between advocates of militancy and those of compromise could produce stalemate and erratic policies in matters affecting Japan. Ultimately, however, the weight of vested interests in modernization and economic development is likely to prevail, provided that Japan's reaction in the interim does not revive the latent fear and distrust that is rooted in historic enmity. Should this occur, a spiral of escalating tension could dominate the debate in Peking, tipping the balance toward "self-reliance" and confrontation in East Asia.

Beyond these bilateral relationships that affect tangible interests of the Chinese or pose constraints on their policies, it is difficult to predict how far the practical approach will temper the theoretical when the two are in sharp conflict. This is particularly true regarding China's general posture toward managing change in cooperation with other states. There is little prospect that in the next five or so years China will assume an open, nonpolemical stance whenever "Soviet revisionism" or "United States imperialism" provides an inviting target for mobilizing Third World unity and opposition. To be sure, when that "world" subdivides into its conflicting interests, as it has regarding the law of the sea, China's choices will become increasingly complicated. In general, however, Peking's representatives are likely to move from one coalition of verbal confrontation to another, alternately attacking "imperialist," "social imperialist," "monopoly capitalist," and "fascist militarist" opponents.

The less tangible the practical consideration, the more influential will be the theoretical factor. It is one thing for policy advocates in Peking to justify a temporary dependence on foreign technology on the basis of its demonstrable contribution to economic and military power. It is quite another thing to argue that China's responsibility is to contribute positively to the search for solutions to war and ways to maintain both peace and stabilized economic development in the international system. Marxist-Maoist theory holds that these problems are inherent in capitalism and that to mitigate their effects is to delay historical progress. In addition to the communist component of ideology, Sinocentrism and the immediate priority of domestic problems are likely to impede substantial Chinese involvement in global problems.

Destalinization and sudden changes in Soviet policy after the dictator's death had a strong impact on Mao, as evidenced by his repeated discussion of the problem in unpublished speeches. Mao left no legacy of hatred and terror comparable to that of Stalin, so his reputation does not risk the same treatment. Nonetheless, his private remarks indicate concern that his theories might suffer equal contempt. While it does seem probable that Mao's world vision will fade gradually, it will not disappear suddenly by denunciation, regardless of how the Peking regime evolves.

Certainly Mao's world view will not be replaced by a wholly different vision in the first years after his death. Changes in some of its aspects will be constrained by Mao's impact on the generation immediately approaching positions of power and by the need for his successors to establish their legitimacy in his name. Thus, ironically, Mao's own dictum of continuing revolution may be undermined in the future by the fact that the course he had set for China before his death will develop a certain inertia that only a Mao could alter.

Whether one ideological aspect or another survives is likely to depend on the strength of particular bureaucratic interests and parts of the society. Mao's insistence on tactical flexibility, for instance, better suits foreign trade than it does propaganda. Militancy meets the needs of revolutionary support but not necessarily those of diplomatic negotiation. Provincial economic managers must rely on assured imports of key machinery and vital metals that in turn require foreign earnings through exports. Political specialists, by contrast, will probably feel less willing to follow the economic plan, particularly if mass indoctrination campaigns require a temporary interruption of production or negotiation of contracts.

A second influence will be the behavior of other "actors" outside China, including governments, various groups of states, international organizations, and traders. Middle Kingdom assumptions of the "barbarian" nature of the external world were convincingly reinforced between 1840 and 1949. Communism did not initiate this suspicion of foreigners, at times bordering on xenophobia and siege mentality. China's interactions over the previous century had already provided ample ground for such attitudes. An awareness of that heritage should alert these various "actors" to the implications of their own behavior, and thus encourage them to help modify over time the impact of past history. However, changes are unlikely to occur quickly.

THREE

Selected Issues

The actual policy priorities in Peking often differ from those assumed by foreign observers. Visitors to China, for instance, find relatively little concern about or interest in the problem of proliferation of nuclear weapons, despite the high level of attention given to the subject elsewhere and its logical importance for the PRC in view of the Indian detonation and the Japanese potential for acquiring nuclear weapons. Conversely, Chinese verbal preoccupation with the inevitability of a third world war contrasts with the relatively sanguine attitude of Western European and American leaders.

The following issues rank high on the agenda of persons focusing on the 1980s in terms of global problems and China's likely relationship to them. Thus they do not necessarily reflect the perspective that may prevail in Peking. The transformation of a social system, for instance, whether "social imperialism" or capitalism, may be of special concern to Chinese policy planners. However, for policy planners in most other nations it is likely to have little interest.

PROLIFERATION OF NUCLEAR AND CONVENTIONAL ARMS

The PRC steadfastly refuses to sign the Non-Proliferation Treaty on the alleged grounds that for the sake of preserving superpower hegemony the treaty unjustly attempts to deny the right of sovereign states to acquire nuclear weapons. However, senior Chinese officials have privately told Americans that China is opposed to nuclear proliferation in principle and will not facilitate it in practice. There is no reason either to doubt that this is actual policy or to expect it to change in the future.

This policy would face a challenge were South Korea to acquire nuclear weapons. Three factors are relevant: first is the need to maintain an arms balance in the peninsula sufficient to deter either side from initiating war in hope of a quick victory; second is the sense of obligation to support an ally; third is Pyongyang's ability to manipulate the Sino-Soviet rivalry as a means of procuring assistance.

All three factors would compel some response from China. However, this response is unlikely to include the transfer of nuclear weapons, much less the facilities for independent production, to North Korean control. Perhaps a strengthened guarantee of nuclear retaliation from Chinese bases could suffice. This guarantee would more than match Seoul's capability and thereby furnish Pyongyang with an explicit nuclear shield. Manipulation of Sino-Soviet rivalry would not push up the bidding since neither Peking nor Moscow wishes to raise the risks of war on the part of the North so long as both are pledged to come to its defense.

The threat that South Korea will acquire nuclear weapons is sufficiently strong to warrant raising the question of China's attitude toward agreements that would preclude that possibility. One such move would be to make the peninsula a nuclear-free zone. At various times in the past, the PRC has supported a nuclear-free zone for Asia and the Pacific Ocean, but never in a plausible context. It has, however, endorsed similar proposals for Latin America and the Indian Ocean. The threat of proliferation in Northeast Asia would evoke serious concern in Peking. While the prospect of Japan's acquiring nuclear weapons remains remote, it, too, could change. An agreement regarding Korea might lead to the complete exclusion of nuclear weapons from the region, including relevant portions of China and the Soviet Union.

Obviously such developments cannot come about so long as Sino-Soviet hostility continues at present levels with neither side willing to agree even to withdraw forces from contested border areas. Yet a détente between Moscow and Peking cannot be ruled out as possible within the next five years. A second obstacle would be inspection. Satellite reconnaissance has reduced this problem to one of marginal concern, however.

Should Japan develop a nuclear capability, a less adequate but still worthwhile alternative would be no-first-use pledges offered either separately or jointly. China's avowal of no-first-use since its initial detonation on October 16, 1964 is consistent and credible. Japan might follow suit. This would open the door to a regional agreement that would include the Soviet Union and the United States. As a first step toward bringing China into an arms control pact with the superpowers, this type of agreement should not be disparaged.

China's interest in SALT accords has so far been purely polemical. Its attack on "superpower hegemony and the arms race" precludes the possibility of its joining Soviet-American discussions. Although rhetorically the PRC will continue to advocate the destruction and prohibition of all nuclear weapons, China in fact sees no likelihood that serious limitations will be imposed on superpower armaments. China's more immediate interests in Korea and Northeast Asia, however, may prompt PRC concessions intended to forestall nuclear proliferation in the area.

Chinese attitudes toward nuclear weapons are difficult to determine. No annual strategic force posture statements emanate from Peking as they do from Washington. No debate over weapons and strategy appears overtly or even obliquely in journals. However, a partial view of PRC policy with respect to the utility of nuclear arms can be obtained by piecing together unpublished statements by Mao and official conversations with visitors to Peking.

Authoritative versions of extended remarks by Mao made between 1955 and 1967 reveal a persistent denial that nuclear weapons were likely to be used in combat. Mao argued that capitalists wage war for material gains. Therefore, in view of the extent to which nuclear weapons destroy industry and resources, he concluded that they existed only for intimidation and bluff. China's acquisition of a credible counterthreat sufficed to meet this need. Mao's war-fighting scenarios did not justify the acquisition of more costly, complex systems that exceed this minimal capability.

Some insight may be gained into Chinese perceptions of nuclear weapons and their utility through analysis of the vocabulary adopted to translate concepts from American strategic analysis. In 1975 an informed Chinese official agreed with this author that the Chinese term used for "deterrence"—which literally translated means "to terrify, to scare"—did not connote the original meaning of threatening unacceptable damage if an attack occurs. However, the official added, "Since your term originated with nuclear weapons whose main purpose is to intimidate, perhaps the Chinese translation is correct after all." The subtlety of this interpretation was consistent with Mao's strategic view.

Similarly, in elaborating on precisely what kind of "world war" was anticipated in Mao's aforementioned statement concerning its likelihood, Chinese officials implied that they expected the conflict to be regional, not global, and conventional, not nuclear. At the same time they recognized the symbolic need to match nuclear threat with a credible retaliatory capability and argued against an American withdrawal from Western Europe. To protect against this contingency, one top official suggested that it might be necessary to have an independent Western European nuclear force.

Another dimension of Chinese attitudes toward nuclear weapons emerged in discussion of no-first-use pledges. A senior statesman proposed to an American delegation that if the United States and the Soviet Union could agree on no-first-use, he personally believed that France would follow suit with China. Although he hastened to add that he saw no serious prospect of his proposal's coming to fruition because of attitudes in Washington and Moscow, the context of his remarks suggested a greater willingness to acquiesce in "superpower collusion in arms agreements" than Peking's public polemic has reflected.

Most observers see a contradiction between China's claim that the Soviet military buildup in Europe provided superiority in conventional weapons power against NATO and its proposal of a no-first-use posture that would remove NATO's nuclear deterrent. From Peking's vantage point, however, the contradiction is more apparent than real. Repeatedly in his private statements Mao dismissed the likelihood that nuclear weapons ever would be used. He insisted that their destructive power dissuaded capitalists from losing the gains of victory by devastating an opponent with nuclear attack. Seen in this light, nuclear weapons are not a credible deterrent against a Soviet invasion of Western Europe. Therefore, Chinese advice to NATO is to strengthen its conventional capability while forswearing the first use of nuclear weapons. Nonetheless, the Chinese urge continued strengthening of nuclear forces for retaliation against a possible Soviet nuclear attack, unlikely as it may be.

China's own nuclear posture is consistent with this general overview. Twelve years after its initial detonation, the PLA had a modest delivery capability in the form of roughly 20 intermediate-range missiles, 50 medium-range missiles, and some 60 TU-16 bombers with ranges of 1,750, 700, and 1,500 miles, respectively. No intercontinental missile had gone into production by 1977, and only the potential for a submarine-borne capability had emerged. While constrained by limited economic, material, and human resources, China could have accomplished considerably more in this time had its nuclear weapons program been given consistently high priority. Even allowing for technical failures and the difficulty of moving from liquid to solid fuels, it appears that China's allocation of resources reflects its calculation that nuclear weapons fill more of a psychological than a strategic need and are not likely to be used in future wars. If this remains Chinese perception and policy over the next decade, the prospects for nuclear weapons agreements in Northeast Asia will be sufficiently promising to deserve serious and continuous study.

The prospects are less promising, however, regarding proliferation of conventional weapons. China's record in this area is one of continuous activity since 1949. The first Indochina war was decided at Dienbienphu by artillery and ammunition that Mao provided to Ho Chi Minh. In the second Indochina war, Peking immediately furnished Hanoi with MIG fighters in response to the first American air attacks following the Gulf of Tonkin incidents in 1964. In 1965–1966, Chinese arsenals completely reequipped the communist guerrillas in South Vietnam with all small weaponry including mortars in order to enable them to cope with the sudden increase in enemy firepower that resulted from the arrival of American combat forces. Again in 1970, when South Vietnamese and American forces swept through communist stockpile areas in Cambodia, Peking publicly pledged to replace all lost equipment at no cost.

When Soviet impatience with North Korea led to a reduced flow of arms in the early 1970s, the Chinese moved to fulfill Korean needs with aircraft, naval, and electronic equipment. Distant Albania survived 15 years of pressure from the Soviet bloc in part because it could count on China for military deliveries. And communist countries were not the only beneficiaries. Pakistan received more advanced Chinese jet fighters in the mid-1960s than did North Vietnam. In 1976, after the United Arab Republic broke its pact with the Soviet Union, Cairo announced Chinese willingness to supply MIG-19 engines. In addition to these states, a host of insurgent movements, communist and otherwise, have drawn on Chinese stockpiles of AK-47s, small arms, grenades, and ammunition. In his 1967 remarks, Mao called for the stamping of all such weapons to indicate their Chinese manufacture, "except in some instances."

To be sure, despite Mao's call for China to "become the arsenal of world revolution," the actual amount of arms transferred pales in comparison with Soviet and American supplies. Both competition and the desire for stature are certain to keep China in the arms transfer business, even were the ideological imperative to "assist oppressed peoples in armed struggle" to fade over the next decade. But this ideological impulse is not likely to wane. It imbues actions that might otherwise require justification according to the crass calculations of power politics with a moral rectitude. It also helps to offset the effect that China's wider range of diplomatic and economic activity in the international system has in blurring its self-proclaimed revolutionary image. For instance, the greater the official interaction with Rangoon, Bangkok, and Kuala Lumpur, the stronger is the argument by vested bureaucratic interests to sustain the trickle of arms to Burmese, Thai, and Malaysian insurgents on grounds of support for Mao's revolutionary vision.

Military assistance to states and to insurgent groups will probably increase over the next decade, thereby ranking China among the world's major suppliers of conventional weapons. However, technological limitations will exclude the possibility of its transferring advanced aircraft, precision-guided missiles, and the most modern weaponry that will be available from the Soviet Union, the United States, and Western Europe. In addition, Peking lacks the logistical capability (except in Southeast Asia) to replace large amounts of destroyed or captured equipment quickly, as Moscow and Washington were able to do in the 1973 Middle East war.

China's ability and willingness to distribute weapons has the greatest potential impact in South and Southeast Asia. So far, however, China's arms transfer policies have done little more than sustain local insurgencies at survival level; except in Indochina, no decisive victory has resulted from Peking's support. There is no reason to believe that this situation will change significantly in the future. Further afield, Chinese training and advice offers African and Latin American groups valuable help. Although technologically less advanced than Soviet or American aid, Chinese aid may be preferred by these groups because of its greater compatibility with local skills and combat needs. Moreover, while the Chinese are not free of racial prejudice, their deliberate emphasis on Afro-Asian-Latin American unity facilitates personal interaction in these areas.

It is impossible to conceive of Chinese participation in any conventional arms control arrangements, except perhaps in Korea. There the possibility exists that an incipient North-South arms race can be checked by agreement among the larger powers that furnish much of the weaponry. Whether tacit or explicit, bilateral or multilateral, such a step would meet the convergent interests of Moscow, Peking, and Washington in maintaining a stable balance of power in the peninsula.

ARMED INTERVENTION AND SUBVERSION

In contrast with its consistent record of arms transfer, China has rarely intervened in armed conflict beyond its borders. The Korean War of 1950–1953, of course, is the most notable example. Although the war was officially celebrated as a victory against the United States plan "to vanquish Korea at one stroke and go ahead further to invade China," its economic and human costs probably reinforced Chinese caution not to repeat that experience unless in response to overriding considerations of national security and interests in adjacent allies. Except for a few days of desultory gunfire across Himalayan passes in 1965, China played no part in the Indian-Pakistani war, nor did it assist beleaguered Bangladesh against the Indian invasion of 1971. The Burmese communists have barely managed to survive, but no PLA forces have come to their rescue, much less provided them with sufficient strength to expand their territorial base on the Chinese border.

The second Indochina war produced a mixed record. On the one hand, no overt Chinese military participation occurred. On the other hand, PLA road-building teams, formally agreed to by the Laotian government in 1964, provided the pretext for a military presence in two provinces adjoining China. For eight years these troops abstained from combat on the side of the Pathet Lao while securing a buffer area against penetration by Royal Lao, Meo, Thai, or remnant Chinese Nationalist forces.

From 1965 to 1968, approximately 50,000 PLA troops, including two to three antiaircraft divisions, railroad engineers, and construction units operated in North Vietnam. They maintained communications routes across the border to defend against bombing by the United States. They built a vast redoubt in the jungle northwest of Hanoi, complete with an 8,000-foot runway, antiaircraft guns revetted into caves on rails, and nearly

200 military structures. They shot down United States aircraft that were attempting to interdict the main rail line from Nanning to Hanoi. In addition they provided a visible token of China's willingness to shed blood on behalf of North Vietman if a "worst case" American invasion eventuated. The Chinese actions undoubtedly bolstered morale and strengthened resistance to Washington's demands.

Yet throughout these years, Chou and other leaders ritualistically insisted that "China does not have a single soldier stationed beyond her borders." This lie was a necessary safeguard against offering a public provocation to which the United States might have felt compelled to respond with force. However, the PLA troops in Laos and North Vietnam effectively deterred American activities by remaining visible to United States aerial reconnaissance and to electronic surveillance of their behavior and their communications with headquarters in China. While American commentators debated whether China would enter the war, Peking's intervention had in fact already occurred, with a restraining effect on Washington's options.

The cases of Korea and Vietnam are distinguished from other opportunities for Chinese intervention by being both communist and contiguous with China. The caution that has been manifest in PRC behavior, the costs of intervention, the complex logistical requirements, and the consequences of potential failure all argue convincingly against the prospect of overt Chinese participation in wars that do not involve a contiguous communist state. Albania, for instance, is too remote for China to provide meaningful assistance in case of invasion. Peking also lacks the means to sustain the PLA in combat in Africa. Covert advisory groups and specialized cadres may accompany arms shipments and financial assistance. However, Angola demonstrated the limited Chinese ability to compete with the Soviet Union's capacity for major intervention.

Even the nearby island archipelago puts the Philippines, Malaysia, and Indonesia beyond the reach of most Chinese military power. With virtually no troop transports and limited amphibious capability, the PLA is severely constrained in the size of forces it can land and sustain. Infiltration of guerrilla units trained on the mainland could occur but would only increase the type of forces already fighting in an insurgency and would not change the situation strategically.

Here ideology provides a constraint. Following Lenin's cue, Mao insisted that "revolution is not for export" and pointed to the Chinese example to prove that "self-reliance" is the only correct path to power. Theory is reinforced by practicality. Indigenous revolts in Southeast Asia would lose local appeal and risk total alienation if they were to relay on overt Chinese intervention. In every country except Singapore, powerful Chinese minorities are the target of suspicion and sometimes hatred because of their commercial activity, which in some instances dominates the economy. Chou En-lai repeatedly assured local leaders that the PRC sought no role for the overseas Chinese other than that of law-abiding citizens in their country of domicile. He also counseled his compatriots abroad accordingly.

Other considerations reinforce this posture of nonintervention. Hungary and Czechoslovakia vividly demonstrated the precariousness of communist rule that rests on foreign intervention. Chinese commentaries on both instances showed that the Soviet lesson was clear in Peking. There is no likelihood that the PLA will emulate the Red Army in forcefully imposing communism on neighboring states. In the unlikely event that anticommunist uprisings in Korea or Vietnam force the local regime to appeal for help, Peking would respond. However, this contingency is so remote as not properly to fall under the purview of this analysis.

Subversion, an activity more elusive than military intervention to identify and evaluate, is the means by which China prefers to promote the revolutionary struggle abroad. Exhortations from Chinese Communist Party (CCP) leaders openly convey congratulations or condolences, depending on the occasion. Laudatory summaries of alleged insurgent successes appear in the public media. Receptions with high officials in Peking bestow prestige on revolutionary delegations. However, these displays are largely symbolic, unsubstantial manifestations of support; while nettlesome to other governments, they do not threaten their rule.

Verbal aid and comfort that is somewhat more annoying to other governments is provided by clandestine radio stations that purport to be run by indigenous insurgents but actually operate from Chinese territory. These stations advocate the armed overthrow of governments with whom Peking ostensibly enjoys friendly relations. Thus the "Voice of the People of Burma" began operations in 1971, the same year that Ne Win made his first state visit to Peking after the Cultural Revolution. Similar facilities exist for the Thai and Malaysian communists. Selected broadcasts are carried, whole or excerpted, in Chinese media.

More material subversive support is provided through training camps in China, logistical aid, money, ammunition, and arms. These efforts have waxed and waned since 1949 but have never reached major proportions. They have nonetheless exacerbated communal conflicts in the sub-Himalayan region of Nepal, India, and Burma. The Burmese Communist Party, for instance, would probably have been wiped out without access to refuge in Chinese territory. Insurgents in northern Thailand also draw support from Peking. But not since Vietnam in 1954 has this help resulted in final victory.

An important constraint on subversion lies in the conflict between diplomatic and revolutionary interests. At the 1955 Bandung conference of Afro-Asian states, Chou En-lai asked a Thai leader why recognition had not been extended and relations were bad. The reply focused on a prominent exiled Thai politician who was being permitted to broadcast attacks from Peking. Chou promised that this practice would stop, and it did. There is some evidence that Bangkok and Peking thereupon secretly concluded an agreement whereby Thailand would not admit American military bases and China would not encourage the communist insurgency. Similarly in 1974–1975, as the PRC moved to establish diplomatic relations with Bangkok and Kuala Lumpur, Thai and Malaysian insurgent radio stations noticeably softened their virulence.

However, these diplomatic and revolutionary interests are not always mutually incompatible. When Thailand permitted the United States to bomb Indochina from clandestine bases in 1964–1965, Foreign Minister Ch'en I openly called for insurgency. The guerrilla force rarely exceeded a thousand or so poorly trained and equipped troops, reflecting the lack of preparation given to "people's war" despite the attention to it in Chinese media. Nevertheless it offered one means of attempting to pressure Thailand to oust the American troops and bases. But when this move finally occurred in 1976, it was more because of Bangkok's concern over Hanoi than because of its concern about Peking. In short, Chinese subversion was never the threat it was made to appear by Thai and American officials. The example illustrates how subversion may be used for various purposes, including influencing local governments rather than aiming for their overthrow.

As with conventional arms transfers, subversion is spurred by competition. In the 1950s the Central Intelligence Agency sought to undermine PRC rule in minority areas such as Tibet and Yunnan province by using Chinese Nationalist personnel and bases in Burma and Thailand. Peking, in its efforts to counter the CIA strategy, pursued defensive as well as offensive ends through subversive action. In the 1970s Chinese authorities saw Soviet penetration of South and Southeast Asia as threatening their influence in the region and ultimately their national security. Overt and covert measures sought to check Moscow's advance. In Thailand, competing communist insurgencies pit Peking against Hanoi.

In sum, subversion is a widespread practice among states, large and small. China is no exception. Ideology, international competition, and bureaucratic interest impel this activity, but it will not expand beyond past levels. Mao's death removes its primary champion, and competing interests—particularly economic dependence on foreign trade—will limit its ability to disrupt state relations.

The vehemence of China's professed support for "people's war" will vary in accordance with shifts of influence among contending factions in Peking. In addition, local insurgents may enjoy greater success at one time or another as their domestic opponents falter or fail, thereby stimulating proclamations of "a new revolutionary era" in Chinese media. In the final analysis, however, subversion is not likely to play a dominant role in policy or to pose a major threat to China's neighboring regimes.

OCEAN RESOURCES

So far the agenda of problems pertinent to consideration of China's role in the 1980s has focused on issues whose duration provides a basis in past behavior for forecasting future probabilities. Moreover, they are issues of considerable immediate salience. The issue of ocean resources, however, falls into a different category, one lacking much precedent and looming low on the political horizon. Nevertheless, its potential for generating conflict, particularly in East Asia, compels its consideration in connection with China's future role. Fishing has long aroused friction in Northeast Asia, with competition among Chinese, Koreans, Japanese, and Soviets a recurrent source of incidents and prolonged negotiation. Yet the question of fishing rights pales into insignificance in comparison with that of access to the continental shelf and its suspected vast reserves of offshore oil.

Resources in the East China and South China seas could be completely controlled by Peking were China to succeed in pressing its maximum claims to full acceptance. Three approaches are available to the PRC. First, the continental shelf extends from China's mainland and reaches to Korea, Japan, and Taiwan. Current conferences may eventually define a new international law of the sea. Meanwhile, many states are acting on the assumption that they have sovereignty over their land mass as it continues under the ocean. Therefore the PRC claim is not unique.

The second approach is based on a new but rapidly spreading assertion of the right to a so-called economic zone of 200 miles, in which the adjacent state has exclusive rights of exploitation that can be enjoyed by others only with express permission. Already enacted into law by the United States, this principle was earlier expounded by Latin American states. PRC support for the Latin American claim stopped short of applying that claim formally to China, but there is ample precedent for its so doing.

This 200-mile economic zone takes on added importance when coupled with the third approach, namely, one based on territorial claims. Such claims have been alluded to above, but they bear more detailed examination in this context. Chinese Communist maps follow Chinese Nationalist precedent in delineating as territorial waters the entire South China Sea periphery adjacent to Vietnam, Malaysia, and the Philippines. This is based on Peking's claim to the numerous small islands, reefs, and shoals that dot the area, chief of which are the Paracels, or Hsishas, in the north; the Spratleys, or Nanshas, in the south; and the Macclesfield Bank, or Chungshas, in the east. Rival Vietnamese claims for the Paracels and Spratleys stem from French cession; a Philippine claim in the Spratleys has been reinforced by construction of a military airstrip. In addition, of course, Peking defines Taiwan as a province of China. Finally, the unpopulated Senkakus, or Tiao Yu Tai—roughly 100 miles northeast of Taiwan—are contested by China and Japan.

Should Peking extend a 200-mile economic zone encompassing all these points, excepting only the 12 miles of territorial waters of adjacent states, the consequences could be serious. Besides the immediate conflict of claims, the South China Sea as well as much of the East China Sea would become a virtual Chinese preserve. This situation would have far-reaching implications for international commerce as well as for fishing and other activities exploiting the resources of the continental shelf.

The combination of approaches and potential claims can affect China's relations with its neighbors in the East Asian arc extending from Korea to Vietnam. Whether China will adopt a common overall strategy or a piecemeal policy that confronts each issue and country separately, and whether these claims will be pursued through unilateral assertion or bilateral negotiation, remains to be seen. However, the mixed record to date suggests that all options are open to the future leadership.

Peking reacted through military means in the Paracels when the then noncommunist regime in Saigon defied its warnings and sent a small naval force there in January 1974. The PLA victory was subsequently amplified in Chinese media as symbolic of PRC determination to recover "every inch of territory and every drop of water" lost to past intruders. More significantly, a literary eulogy of the event which was widely disseminated in China during the following two years specifically referred to undersea oil as being at stake in the clash and implicitly attacked the United

States as the real opponent. This eulogy was the most militaristic and chauvinistic since the articles that appeared subsequent to the Sino-Soviet border clashes of 1969.

Contrary to this precedent, however, was China's implied willingness to compromise, which was signaled in Peking's response to Philippine offshore oil efforts. In 1976 Manila announced that foreign concessions would explore the Reed Bank near the Spratleys, whereupon Saigon (then communist) and Taipei protested. Peking followed suit. The Philippine foreign minister then claimed that China's protest ought not to be taken seriously because President Marcos had already informed top Chinese officials of his intentions during his 1975 state visit. According to his account, their attitude at that time implied acquiescence.

The context of these two incidents is worth noting. In the first case, a communist take-over of Saigon was imminent. If Chinese claims were to be made good by the use of force, action would have to be taken quickly against a legitimate enemy; delay would have meant confronting an official friend. By contrast, Mao's meeting with Marcos climaxed a long effort at winning Philippine recognition. The Reed Bank concession was not so valuable or special that it warranted armed confrontation.

Thus the choice between military confrontation and compromise through diplomacy can be affected by the behavior of foreign powers. President Thieu moved provocatively; President Marcos showed tact. Overt challenge, particularly in defiance of specific warnings, can create unity where none exists. China is not unique in this respect. Private exchanges well in advance of action may prove especially salutary in that they acknowledge the PRC position in principle in order to elicit compromise in practice.

The Senkaku Islands are suggestive in this regard. In 1970 Japanese patrols harassed Taiwanese fishermen in adjacent waters. Unprecedented student demonstrations in Taipei triggered sympathetic reactions among Chinese in Hong Kong and the United States. Chiang's government protested to Tokyo. Meanwhile, PRC propaganda whipped up a short-lived campaign over the islands which soon subsided in anticipation of Prime

Minister Tanaka's visit to normalize relations in 1972. Chinese officials privately assured their Japanese counterparts that the issue had been "shelved" for the sake of better ties. It appeared that Peking's position was initially determined by Taipei's handling of the matter and subsequently changed to take advantage of Japanese reaction to the "Nixon shock" of détente with China. For its part, Washington took a neutral stance and warned American firms against exploring for offshore oil in this area on behalf of any contending country.

The Senkaku issue remains dormant, but it may not be dead. In 1974, Vice-Premier Teng Hsiao-p'ing privately indicated to a visiting delegation of overseas Chinese that the controversy had been quieted for tactical reasons. He added that it was complicated by the question of Taiwan and warned his audience that it would return to prominence at some future time. These tactics could parallel Peking's handling of disputed Sino-Indian border claims. In 1954 Prime Minister Nehru queried Chou En-lai about conflicting maps printed in the two capitals. Chou said it was not necessary to discuss the matter at that time, and the two leaders signed an agreement on the Five Principles of Peaceful Coexistence. China subsequently built a strategic road through contended territory in the western sector linking Sinkiang with Tibet. Announcement of this project prompted Indian patrols in the region, a PLA seizure and expulsion of the troops, and a formal protest from Nehru in 1958. Chou then denied that the matter required discussion, since presence of the road determined ownership in favor of China.

Whether Peking will reopen the Senkaku issue when its political or military posture makes such an act convenient cannot be determined so long as formal agreement has not been reached between China and Japan. Taipei's exploitation of the issue as a symbol of Chinese sovereignty constrains Peking's willingness to cede the island outright. More important, of course, will be the general development of Sino-Japanese relations. Also relevant will be the impact of China's posture on Soviet-Japanese relations, where Moscow's retention of four small islands north of Hokkaido remains a sore point. Finally, domestic politics in Japan, as in China, can make territorial compromise impossible. The overall risks of intransigence so far outweigh the importance of the islands that it seems unlikely that Peking will press the point. Nonetheless, the issue has the potential for exploitation either to influence Tokyo on other matters or to affect domestic Chinese politics.

The continental shelf poses a far more complex and explosive problem. Here the PRC position to date is ambiguous but encouraging of future compromise. In December 1970, *Peking Review* took the unusual step of reprinting an article by John Gittings, a British scholar, which urged that undersea access be "apportioned by mutual agreement as has been done in the North Sea." Then in 1973 the PRC officially protested against American companies that were exploring the Yellow and East China seas with South Korean approval by noting that "areas of jurisdiction for China and her neighbors in the Yellow and East China Sea have not yet been delimited." Again in 1974 the Chinese Ministry of Foreign Affairs objected to an agreement between Seoul and Tokyo concerning joint use of the shelf between South Korea and Japan. Terming the pact an "infringement of Chinese sovereignty" that the PRC "absolutely cannot accept," the note then called for consultation with "the other countries concerned."[1] This statement not only signaled potential compromise, but also implied de facto acceptance of the South Korean regime.

This implication of de facto acceptance of the South raises the question of the status of North Korea, whose need for oil and foreign exchange is as great as that of the other states in the area. In 1975 Peking's more militant posture was marked by Chinese acknowledgment of Pyongyang as the only legitimate government in the peninsula. Certainly, the willingness and ability of the Chinese to influence Vietnamese and North Korean behavior will remain sensitive to Soviet competition for some time to come. Moscow assiduously exploited conflicting claims to the Paracels and Spratleys in order to exacerbate Sino-Vietnamese relations. It would similarly exploit any parallel opportunity regarding the continental shelf. Thus Chinese considerations must take Korea into account in addition to Japan.

Global agreement on a new law of the sea would finesse most of

[1] *Peking Review*, no. 6, Feb. 8, 1974, p.3.

these problems. In its absence, however, the regional situation requires delicate handling if political confrontation and military conflict are to be avoided. The stakes are high. Over the next 25 years offshore oil could provide important relief for energy needs in Korea, Japan, Taiwan, and the Philippines. The possibility that natural gas deposits could also be tapped would add to the potential riches. Although this relief is not essential for China, which has considerable onshore oil and the third largest coal reserves in the world, the continental shelf holdings could relieve foreign exchange constraints on major imports of whole plants and technology. They could also provide leverage over China's neighbors, particularly Japan. Finally, they might provide a necessary reserve for the staggering needs of an industrialized mainland in the twenty-first century.

It is impossible to grasp the full magnitude of the issue of the continental shelf until several years' systematic exploration determines the actual offshore potential. Foreign speculation explains Peking's ambiguous but seemingly compromising posture as designed to permit this exploration at no cost to China until evidence confirms the existence of oil, at which time PRC positions will harden. Although logical in the abstract, this theory ignores the variables, internal and external, that have been identified above. It also assumes more continuity in policy making and implementation than seems likely in view of the changes of leadership that are bound to occur. Finally, China's interaction with the relevant governments in the interim may affect the leadership composition and the attitudes in Peking in ways that would make negotiated compromise more or less likely.

Because Japan looms so large in Chinese calculations, a brief review of its options is in order. Dependency can be double-ended. Just as leaders in Peking will argue over the ideological propriety and practical wisdom of tying a major share of energy exports and technology imports to Japan, so, too, policy makers in Tokyo will focus on the implications of relying on mainland sources of oil, coal, and ultimately natural gas. Aside from purely economic questions of the costs of refining Chinese crude oil, with its low-sulfur, high-paraffin content, and the advantages of competitive bargaining among several suppliers,

Japan must confront the question of reliability. Chinese productivity might be disrupted by domestic political turmoil of the sort that occurred during the Cultural Revolution and to a lesser degree in the aftermath of Chou En-lai's death. Deliveries might be deliberately discontinued as a result of decisions in the economic or foreign policy spheres. Consequently, alternative sources in the Soviet Union, Indonesia, Algeria, and the Middle East will remain attractive. It is worth noting that whereas Sino-Japanese discussions in 1974 of a long-term agreement ranged between estimates of 30 and 50 million tons of oil as a target for 1980, by 1976 those figures had dwindled—through the initiation of Japan—to between 15 and 18 million tons.

Projecting 25 years ahead requires differing estimates depending upon alternative assumptions concerning the Chinese willingness to mortgage future oil earnings in order to finance large imports of the advanced technology necessary for exploitation of deeper waters beyond the Po Hai gulf. This willingness already became a politically charged issue in the mid-1970s. Should China decide to move in the direction of such mortgages, it will not be the only country to do so. It will thus be competing for scarce and complex drilling equipment. It will also need time to investigate, negotiate, and provide the bureaucratic and material infrastructure to handle extensive offshore oil exploitation.

The problem of ocean resources transcends Chinese policy and East Asia. Its resolution is intimately related to global law, organization, and resource management. Whereas the prospects are slim and the utility is marginal for involving China in arms control negotiations or accords, PRC policy will still significantly affect international policy regarding ocean resources. The current Chinese political situation is unpromising in terms of Peking's actual interest in negotiating compromise solutions to the problem. However, other states should act so as not to prejudice the possibility of a positive change of attitude in Peking. If and when this change eventuates, they should initiate a deliberate and systematic discussion of the issue and its implications with Chinese officials.

CHINA'S PLACE IN THE WORLD

The "Middle Kingdom" label no longer applies to China. Nevertheless, observers seem compelled to fix China's place in the world in terms of relatively new nomenclature, such as "East-West" or "North-South." But when "East" connoted a monolithic Soviet-led bloc confronting an American alliance system, the label was inappropriate and short-lived. And if "North" connotes modern industrialized and politically developed states as opposed to the less developed societies of the "South," these categories are equally inapplicable to China.

The widely accepted North-South dichotomy, however, is a useful political shorthand to which China's relationship should be further considered. First, it must be clear why too literal an acceptance of this terminology obscures an understanding of China's situation, as perceived by both China's leaders and independent observers. Politically speaking, China is the oldest and largest society in the world with a governmental heritage that spans millenia. Western criteria of political modernization may give it low marks in terms of institutionalized decision making, conflict resolution, and rational resource allocation. But the fact remains that Chinese communist society, with its total political direction, has been disciplined, purposeful, industrious, frugal, self-confident, conscious of identity and unity, and committed to an egalitarian ethic.

One or more of these societal characteristics may exist elsewhere, but nowhere in the less developed world do all exist in combination. This accounts for the ability of China's system to cope with economic problems that in terms of sheer magnitude have no equal, except perhaps in India. The imperial Chinese system collapsed under the weight of internal and external challenges. Nearly 40 years of intermittent interregnum, invasion, and civil war ended in 1949. A new political system combined an all-encompassing ideology with an ability to mobilize and manage people, resources, and institutions. The result was to lift the nation from abject poverty and political paralysis to living standards minimally consonant with self-respect and to power adequate to win the respect of other states.

Selected indicators of growth and forecasts of bottlenecks cloud the prospects for the next 25 years, but compared with most of the world's less developed economies, China stands high on the slope between the valley of despair and the peak of achievement. No one can deny the extremely low standard of living that prevails throughout the countryside, the tremendous pressure of population on resources, the scarcity of land for cultivation, and the problems of urbanization and modernization. When Chinese officials forswear any intention of becoming a superpower and insist that their country is "poor and backward," they are appropriately realistic and modest. But to take these assertions as proof of China's parity with the majority of states in Asia, Africa, and Latin America that are conventionally lumped together as South or Third World is to distort beyond all recognition not only the Chinese self-image but also China's potential role.

For various reasons, the PRC seeks to have the best of an identification with both North and South. Political parity with the established elite in the international system has numerous rewards, both psychic and tangible. Chinese leaders offer counsel on European security matters, meeting their French and British counterparts as equals. Trade with Western Europe taps technology and markets. The power balance with the Soviet Union is more easily handled multilaterally than bilaterally. These same considerations apply to Chinese interactions with Japan and the United States. In short, the Northern club has a new member, even if it does not make all the meetings.

At the same time, the PRC maintains its ability to identify credibly with the South on grounds of a common level of economic development, an allegedly similar heritage of foreign exploitation, and a united struggle against the superpowers. In addition, it has in some instances utilized an explicit revolutionary appeal; in other cases it has taken advantage of a racial consciousness that derives from centuries of white imperialism over the peoples of Asia, Africa, and Latin America. Thus Peking's international role from 1949 to the present has been directed as much as possible at extending China's influence throughout the countries successively identified as Afro-Asian and Third World. Numerous failures accompany notable

71

successes. Yet China's identification with the South remains firmly established in the minds of many Chinese as well as key foreign audiences, regardless of the degree to which these perceptions do not coincide with actual states of affairs.

During the next 10 years the tension between the North and South orientations is certain to grow as China increases its interaction with and dependence on advanced industrial states while espousing Third World positions in international forums. Already certain dichotomies and paradoxes are evident. Publicly, Peking's leaders decry Malthusian prognoses and champion the principle of increased productivity rather than that of decreased birthrates. Privately they seek the latest information on birth control and share their own considerable wealth of experience and knowledge in this area. Chinese statements laud OPEC's use of oil as a weapon in the Middle East struggle and call on other resource-rich, capital-poor countries to join in common cause to "change the international system." Yet the PRC refuses to join OPEC and shows no intention of entering into multilateral production or pricing agreements.

According to Mao's theory, "contradiction" is natural in the course of foreign affairs. In practice, however, the tension between China's two orientations is likely to be resolved by a gradual, subtle shift away from the South and toward the North. The rate and extent of this shift will depend in part on how vested interests in China come to see the utility of pursuing economic development through relationships with the advanced industrial states in comparison with the interests that would be served by alignment with the poorer countries. The trend since 1970 has been toward compromise with the North and away from confrontation, as evidenced both by Peking's approval of a "dialogue" between the Second and Third Worlds and by PRC relations with the European Economic Community and West Germany.

The PRC posture will also depend on how the North deals with China. Parallels with the past run the risk of oversimplification and obfuscation. Nevertheless it is useful to recall the case of Japan. At the turn of the century, this small Asian nation ended 30 years of social, economic, and political self-transformation in order to identify itself with the North of the time—the European imperialist powers. As if to prove the point, it whipped Russia, the largest if not the strongest member of the club.

Japan won acceptance as a member of the North, but on a limited basis and accompanied by slights that suggested inferior status and took on added significance because of its sense of racial alienation. In the next half-century, Japan pursued goals of national security, economic stability, and international identity similar to those of other imperialist powers. But mutual miscalculation resulted in a disastrous war. Finally a successful peace arrangement led to the complete integration of Japan into the international system and allowed it to advance its interests in harmony with those of other members.

China took much longer to reorient itself when the international system ended its isolation in the nineteenth century. Then in 1949 a "new China" demanded acceptance explicitly on its own terms, although it implicitly accepted most of the system's rules. The response was rejection and exclusion from that part of the system dominated by the United States, initially on a temporary basis, but after PRC entry into the Korean War, on an avowedly permanent basis. China was still able to participate in important ways in the part of the system under Soviet domination, but Mao eventually determined that this type of engagement was too confining and threatened his socioeconomic goals. He saw the former colonial world as offering an inviting Afro-Asian alternative, but it quickly proved to lack the necessary coherence and strength to survive as an organized political system. Meanwhile, China declared itself opposed to both the American and Soviet subsystems and searched for ways to weave new ties with disgruntled members, such as France and Rumania, and Afro-Asian cohorts, such as Indonesia and Cambodia.

The parallel between Japan and China breaks down at many points, of course, although paradoxically some of the "negative" differences have "positive" implications. For example, Japan played by the rules of the imperialist system and conquered much of Asia. China disavowed the rules of the capitalist system but shows no aggressive designs against its neighbors. Japan was wholly dependent on the system yet attacked its dominant members. China is largely self-sufficient but has not sought hegemony over more vulnerable countries.

The significance of the analogy lies in the apparent difficulty with which the prevailing powers in the system expand their membership and accept changes in status, power, and process. Misperception and miscalculation obstruct accommodation. War can block it altogether, although in the case of Japan that blockage proved short-lived. By 1980, 31 years will have elapsed since the establishment of the People's Republic of China. This period should have provided more than sufficient opportunity for China and the superpowers to determine the relationship among them most satisfactory to all. However, the United States spent two-thirds of this time denying China's credentials and defending its own portion of the international system against the new member's alleged threat. The Soviet Union spent an almost equal amount of time in an effort that both paralleled and for a while overlapped the American effort. Meanwhile, China's ability to adapt itself to a new role in the international system was partially paralyzed by a perceived threat from one or the other superpower, and for a brief period from both simultaneously. Also basic to this entire period was the earlier trauma of successive losses of territory and status as imperial China collapsed and successor regimes failed to cope with internal decay and foreign deprivations.

The danger, therefore, lies in expecting too much accommodation too fast. China's role cannot be predetermined and imposed by others. China's relationships with the North and the South cannot be prescribed or proscribed. China fits incompletely in both clubs by inclination and by constitution. However, the ease, speed, and extent of China's association with the North depends critically on how the various nations and institutions of the North deal with China, rather than how it deals with them. The post-Mao years will shape the next generations of leadership, their perceptions, and their expectations. Political preoccupations will still be domestic. Foreign policy will result more from reactions to events than from initiation of them. Weeds of confrontation will compete with seeds of cooperation for growth. A principal objective of the dominant members of the international system must be to influence Chinese visions and policies toward compromise and convergence on the key issues that require regional and global participation by the PRC.

This task may require a greater degree of patience and persistence than is available or likely, particularly from the Soviet Union. The alternatives, however, are far more exigent in the long run. China may exert its growing strength to shape its own subsystem within the South against the North. Or it may act on its own in angry, frustrated isolation with a growing potential for disruption due to ambition, desperation, or both. The 1970s have begun the process of mutual accommodation. The 1980s must complete this process before that potential becomes a real threat.

Selected Bibliography

Barnett, A. Doak: *Uncertain Passage: China's Transition to the Post-Mao Era*, Brookings Institution, Washington D.C., 1974.

Chiu, Hungdah, ed.: *China and The Question of Taiwan: Documents and Analysis*, Praeger Publishers, Inc., New York, 1973.

Clough, Ralph N., A. Doak Barnett, Morton H. Halperin, and Jerome A. Cohen: *The U.S., China, and Arms Control,* Brookings Institution, Washington, D.C., 1975.

Clubb, Oliver Edmund: *China and Russia: The "Great Game,"* Columbia University Press, New York, 1971.

Cohen, Jerome A., and Hungdah Chiu: *People's China and International Law: A Documentary Study*, Princeton University Press, Princeton, N.J., 1974.

Fitzgerald, Stephen: *China and the Overseas Chinese*, Cambridge University Press, New York, 1972.

Gittings, John: *The World and China, 1922–1973,* Harper and Row, New York, 1974.

Hsiung, James Chieh: *Law and Policy in China's Foreign Relations*, Columbia University Press, New York, 1972.

Larkin, Bruce D.: *China and Africa, 1949–1970*, University of California Press, Berkeley, Calif., 1971

Taylor, Jay: *China and Southeast Asia: Peking's Relations with Revolutionary Movements*, Praeger Publishers, Inc., New York, 1974.

China's Economic Future

Robert F. Dernberger

ONE

Introduction: Forecasting China's Economy

The emergence of the People's Republic of China as a major world power over the past quarter-century already has done much to alter the international system. China's economic evolution and its interaction with Chinese politics can be expected to play a major role in the future of both China and the world. Although not the most powerful nation in terms of military or economic strength, China certainly is the largest, with a population accounting for approximately one out of every four people. In addition, even though China accurately can be classified as an underdeveloped country—its per capita Gross National Product (GNP) is approximately 250 U.S. dollars—and does not possess the sophisticated weaponry to be ranked as a "superpower," the importance of China's international role is most readily indicated by its rank as the sixth largest producer of goods and services in the world, the largest producer of machine tools, and the nation with the third largest annual expenditures on defense. The purpose of this study is to forecast—i.e., to present the range of most likely outcomes concerning—China's economic evolution over the next 10 to 15 years, its interaction with Chinese politics, and the possible impact of that interaction on the international system.

China's future is unlikely to be a simple projection of past trends or to be accurately estimated by means of an econometric model based on past developments. Although influenced by and, to some extent at least, based upon the legacy of the past, developments in China over the past quarter-century reveal one of the most radical, massive, and sweeping social-economic and political experiments in the history of the world. To compound the problem faced in discussing China's future, in the late 1950s a cloak of secrecy was placed on quantitative information concerning economic activity in China. This cloak of secrecy has been partially lifted in recent years, but detailed quantitative analysis of the Chinese economy still must rely on the difficult "art" of piecing together fragmentary bits of evidence with the help of "heroic" assumptions to provide the necessary "guesstimates."

The dynamic changes occurring in the economic and political situation in China and our lack of information concerning them preclude the use of a sophisticated econometric model in forecasting future developments, and present serious difficulties for an attempt to use a simple, but more relevant, approach as well. For example, the attempt to derive trends based on the economic performance of the last quarter-century is complicated by the fact that the lack of stability in that period's economic growth and structural change makes it very difficult to identify trends for the period as a whole or even for a typical sequence of its years. Quite simply, how can we hope to determine a "normal" trend during a period that included the impact on the economy of the land reform and postwar rehabilitation (1949–1952), the Korean War (1950–1953), the introduction of Soviet planning and the First Five Year Plan (1953–1957), the collectivization of agriculture (mid-1950s), the decentralization of the management of the economy (1957–1958), the Great Leap and Commune Movement (1958–1959), the agricultural crisis (1959–1961), the recovery after the crisis (1962–1965), the Cultural Revolution (1965–1967), the implementation of radical economic programs (late 1960s), the reemergence of moderate economic programs and the large-scale purchases of foreign plants and technology (1970s), and the deaths of Mao Tse-tung, Chou En-lai, and Chu Teh in a single year (1976)?

This instability is partly a result of the structure of the Chinese economy, which causes even more difficulties for the task of forecasting. Unlike those in the United States, economic activities in China are not the results of individual decisions that are motivated by a desire to maximize profits or to increase self-satisfaction. Rather, they are influenced to a great extent by a bureaucratic decision-making network that operates at all economic levels, although allowances must be made for considerable "slippage" between administrative instructions and actual results. Furthermore, the decisions made regarding economic activities reflect the combined consideration of the whole complex of short- and long-run, private and social, economic and political objectives held by the decision makers.

Economic systems of this type are often called *command economies*, but the Chinese economic system differs from the typical command economy in three important respects. First, there is much greater initiative from "below," insofar as there is more interaction between those outside and those within the administrative bureaucracy. Second, there is much less routinization and fewer standard practices in the operation of the system; problem solving is accomplished through consultation and negotiation—playing it by ear—rather than through a set pattern of rules and procedures. Finally, many decisions are made at the lower levels of the bureaucracy. In any event, the particular economic policies that lead to economic activities result from a consideration of many factors (many of which cannot be easily weighed in monetary terms) through a process of interaction among decision makers at various levels both inside and outside the administrative system. Thus it is very difficult to unravel accurately the particular considerations and decision-making processes that lead to a given economic result.

More problematical in an attempt to project the future is the remarkable willingness of the Chinese to change economic policies quickly and frequently when particular difficulties are encountered or earlier policies prove unsatisfactory, and to experiment with unprecedented and rather radical policies. The only operation constraints on the decision makers appear to be those that are rather broadly defined by their ideology, such as the prohibition on reintroducing private property, free markets, and profit maximization as the principal means for determining the allocation of commodities and resources. These frequent changes in policy are explained by the Chinese as a reflection of their belief that theory should come from practice. Since the Chinese think that purely economic problems do not exist, they see reliance on static, purely economic theories as unacceptable and doomed never to lead to solutions to complex social-economic-political problems. Often the emphasis on "learning by doing" is somewhat costly in economic terms alone, for the Chinese are willing to sacrifice purely economic gains for the achievement of a broader set of objectives.

A final complication is the difficulty of identifying the decision makers and the process by which decisions are made, not only at the upper levels of the political hierarchy but at all levels of the economic system. Within the production unit itself (i.e., the factory in industry or the production team in agriculture), there are the questions of who the decision makers are, what their objectives are, what instructions they receive and how they interpret them, how much interaction occurs between these decision makers and the masses, and what effect this has on the decisions made. The same questions could be asked about the political and economic decision makers at the county level, the municipal level, the provincial level, and in Peking. Each participant in this decision-making network has, of course, an individual set of objectives and long-run goals. Indeed, the history of the last quarter-century shows that considerable differences exist over economic policies. These are not just the basic ideological disputes between the more radical and the more moderate approaches; they also include differences over specific policies, such as the role of foreign trade, pace of collectivization, mechanization of agriculture, investment in heavy industry, role of markets, property ownership, wages, and decentralization of decision making. The remarkable durability of the Chinese system—until today, at least—is the result of the leadership's ability to formulate workable compromises that often are dictated by economic reality. Nonetheless, these compromises are somewhat unstable; underlying ideological differences over economic policy could erupt openly at any time and lead to rather sudden and extensive changes in economic policies and institutions.

There is no need to belabor this point. The above review should be sufficient to indicate the hazards involved in any attempt to delineate the range of most likely developments in China's economic future and their impact on the international system. Why, then, attempt such a forecast at all? The answer is simple: Difficult and tentative answers to important questions are much more useful than easy answers to trivial questions.

* * * * * * * * *

In reading my arguments, some readers may well wonder whether this study was written before or after Mao's death. The essay was drafted, presented to a workshop at the Council on Foreign Relations in New York, and revised in light of the helpful criticisms and suggestions I received there before Mao died. The final revisions before publication were made immediately following Mao's death. At that time, a careful rereading convinced me that no significant changes in my argument were desirable.

As this study goes to press, reports are being published of a major purge of the "radicals" by the "moderate" forces, apparently brought on by either the radicals' attempt to seize the opportunity provided by Mao's death to expand their own power or the moderates' knowledge that they could expand their own power once the radicals could no longer rely on a live Mao for support. Although there is good reason for believing these reports, no one knows enough of the facts to understand the purge fully, and it will probably be some time before anyone knows not only the facts but also—and more important—their cause and effect. Nonetheless, what is reported to have happened thus far would require no revisions to be made in my arguments; in fact, these events only strengthen my analysis. While the possibility of a takeover by the radicals is now even less likely than I had allowed for, much more important is the increased probability that my forecast of stable economic growth and the moderate foreign policy behavior such growth is likely to engender will prove accurate.

Nonetheless, the many qualifications to my conclusions and the possible alternative developments discussed in Chapters

Five and Six must be included for consideration. The "moderates," even if they succeed in gaining complete control of China, *are not* followers of the Chicago School of Economics or firm believers in laissez faire free enterprise. Furthermore, even if the current holders of power in China who are described as "radicals" are removed from power, the appeal to the cause of "radicalism" that is embodied in the works of Mao, the ideological father of Chinese Communism, will not be eliminated. Therefore, I stand by the arguments presented below, now that Mao is dead, somewhat more strongly than I did when they were written, before he died.

TWO

Past Performance and Present State of China's Economy

During a very few years after the Second World War, the Chinese Communists emerged from their guerrilla bases, rapidly seized control of large portions of Manchuria and North China, crossed the Yangtze, swept through the south, and in 1949 announced the creation of their new government for all China—the People's Republic of China. The economy they inherited included over 500 million people who were poorly fed, clothed, and housed and who had a per capita GNP that was probably less than 50 U.S. dollars. The economy's productive capacity had suffered severe damage during the Civil War. Moreover, after the Second World War the Russians had dismantled and removed over 50 percent of the industrial capital in China's largest industrial and railroad base, Manchuria. Even in the 1930s, industrial output had accounted for only 10 percent of China's GNP, but in 1949 the absolute level of output in industry fell to only one-half its prewar peak. That same year was little better for agriculture: grain and cotton outputs were, respectively, about 25 and 50 percent lower than the prewar peak levels.

In addition to commodities production being at a very low level, the underdeveloped and partially destroyed transportation system made regional distribution of both goods needed for production and processed goods a serious problem. The rampant inflation that had been under way since 1936 had also seriously distorted business incentives (by leading to speculation, etc.) and had prevented the "rational" allocation of resources to meet China's basic needs ("rational" being the use of resources in their most effective and beneficial way, which by definition can occur only in a noninflationary economy). Moreover, with domestic shortages limiting China's export capacity, the state treasury's holdings of foreign exchange reserves having been removed by Chiang Kai-shek to Taiwan, and the likelihood being small of foreign aid and assistance from a hostile Western world, China's capacity for alleviating those shortages by imports was severely limited.

The length and scope of this analysis do not permit a description of how skillfully fiscal and monetary policies were used in the reconstruction program that restored production to its peak levels of the prewar period by 1952. Those enterprises that had been owned by the Nationalist government or by "bureaucratic" capitalists were taken over by the state, but private enterprise was allowed to remain in operation, as was a market system for the allocation of resources. The state budget was balanced, and revenues were used for investment in the public sector. State trading companies were created to dominate both internal and external trade in key commodities, but rationing was not yet introduced, nor were price controls. Furthermore, this remarkably successful rehabilitation program was carried out with limited Soviet aid while China was fighting the world's largest military power in the Korean War and at the same time carrying out a sweeping redistribution of economic, social, and political power by means of land reform in the countryside.

Between 1949 and 1952, the new government restored price stability, increased industrial output 2.5-fold and agricultural output by 50 percent, brought the balance of payments under control, and more than doubled imports (with producer goods accounting for over 90 percent of the total imports). Most important, GNP per capita (in real terms) in 1952 was 35 percent higher than it was in 1936.[1]

[1] State Statistical Bureau, *Ten Great Years*, Foreign Language Press, Peking, 1960.

INSTITUTIONAL REORGANIZATION
OF THE ECONOMY

Having successfully consolidated their control over the population and economy and revived production to roughly the levels attained before the war, the Chinese Communists launched their program of institutional change and economic development to achieve the transformation of China into a modern industrial power. They rapidly socialized agricultural production by introducing elementary producers' cooperatives in the early 1950s, advanced producers' cooperatives in the mid-1950s, and the People's Communes in 1958.[2] The People's Communes, which were very large, were expected to replace the county-level government administration and led to excessively centralized decision making concerning production and allocation in Chinese agriculture. This situation compounded the difficulties the Chinese had in coping with the agricultural crises following the Great Leap Forward in 1958, which were caused partly by bad weather. Thus, in the early 1960s the Chinese reduced the size of communes, returned governmental administrative duties to the county governments, and restored considerable production and allocation responsibilities to the "teams" (the equivalent of the earlier elementary producers' cooperatives). In recent years,

---

[2]The number of elementary producers' cooperatives increased from 3,600 in 1952 to 633,000 in 1955, advanced producer's cooperatives increased from 500 in 1955 to 682,000 in 1957, and People's Communes grew from none in 1957 to 680,000 in 1958. By 1958, 97 percent of the peasant households in China were members of socialist agricultural units. Each successive change in organization introduced a larger unit that absorbed those already in existence: the elementary producers' cooperatives contained 30 to 40 households, the advanced producers' cooperatives contained 200 to 300 households (with brigades equivalent in size to the former elementary producers' cooperatives and teams equivalent in size to the traditional mutual aid teams) and the People's Communes contained 5,000 to 8,000 households (with brigades equivalent in size to the former advanced producers' cooperatives and teams equivalent in size to the former elementary producers' cooperatives). See Kenneth R. Walker, *Planning in Chinese Agriculture,* Aldine, Chicago, 1965.

there has been some indication that these teams are losing some of this power to the "brigades" (equivalent in size to the earlier advanced producers' cooperatives) and that—with the spread of rural, small-scale industries and farmland reconstruction, including irrigation projects that are under commune control—the commune itself is becoming a more important production and allocative unit. Despite these shifts in the locus of decision-making power, Chinese agricultural production has been organized under cooperative ownership over the past two decades and can be expected to remain so in the near future.[3]

In industry, state ownership was already significant in 1952 (accounting for over 50 percent of the gross value of industrial output) because of the takeover of enterprises formerly owned and operated by the Nationalist government and the bureaucratic capitalists who had ties to that government. Although allowed to remain in operation, private enterprise was subject to numerous taxes, fines, and labor union problems; it relied heavily on the state's orders for output and allocation of inputs. Many private capitalists took advantage of the state's offer to buy them out with bonds equal to half the value of their capital assets and jobs as plant managers.[4] In 1952, 5 percent of the gross value of industrial output came from these joint state-private enterprises, but this share increased to over 30 percent by 1956, when all private industrial enterprises had been absorbed into the socialist sector.

Ownership and control of these state enterprises was highly centralized under the economic ministries of the central government in the 1950s, and the directives concerning the

[3] The production units—communes, brigades, and teams— in the cooperative sector are not integrated into the detailed state plan. They determine their own production plans, are allocated inputs by the state, pay taxes and sell goods under negotiated contracts to the state, and distribute income to their members. Individual households are allocated small private plots and can consume or sell the output of these plots in rural markets that exist for that purpose. Key commodities, however, must be sold to the state trading companies. State farms do exist and are the most mechanized in China. Nonetheless, they are not very important in terms of either total acreage or productivity and are not expanding, except in the limited areas being newly developed for farming.

[4] A fixed interest rate of 6 percent was originally paid to the former owners of these plants, but this policy was discontinued in the 1960s.

allocation of their outputs and inputs were derived from the state's economic plan. Considerable decentralization has occurred since the 1950s; today only key industrial enterprises are directly under the control of the central government, and the largest of the remaining enterprises are operated by provincial and municipal governments. Rural, small-scale industries are managed by the county governments. The allocative decisions for all these plants, whatever level of government owns and operates them, are now incorporated into the state economic plan and are subject to the approval of higher-level authorities. This hierarchy of state enterprises in the socialist sector and commune-operated plants in the cooperative sector will likely remain as a fundamental characteristic of China's economy.

In the absence of a market system for allocation and with industrial enterprises run by state-appointed managers whose objective is not to maximize profit, allocation is based on administrative decisions and directives that are incorporated in a state plan. These result from negotiations among economic units at various levels, but the central government ultimately exercises considerable control. Although the Chinese originally attempted to introduce the highly formalized and centralized Soviet system of planning in the 1950s, they have instead adopted a much less formalized and more decentralized system. The Chinese realized how difficult it would be to derive in Peking consistent and efficient allocative plans for all industrial activity; at the same time, they wanted to increase the participation of "the masses" in the decision-making process. Currently, the state's economic plans in industry are the cumulation of decisions made at various levels, with considerable initiative coming from lower levels. Thus, although the central government retains the power of final approval, Chinese planning relies on considerable flexibility and initiative in problem solving at lower levels. This feature of Chinese planning has become and is likely to remain a unique and important feature of China's economic system.

The central planning authorities, of course, are not passive participants in the process of resource allocation, exercising their veto power in reaction to the requests and suggestions they receive "from below." They directly control and operate key industries, the transportation network, and internal trade in key commodities and all external trade (through their direct control and operation of the state trading network). Especially important is Peking's ability to restructure the economy by its direct control over most investment. Profits of state enterprises—except for limited earnings that are retained by those enterprises for working capital, workers' fringe benefits, and small investment projects—are transferred to the budget of the government level that controls the enterprises.[5] Although these revenues are collected by counties, provinces, municipalities, and the state in their respective budgets, the budgets of these units are incorporated into the state's budget and the central government severely limits the discretionary ability of the lower levels to spend the revenue they collect. At the same time, the total revenues that are combined in the state's budget give Peking considerable ability—after allowing for expenditures on government administration, defense, and social welfare—to divert profits of state enterprises collected in one sector or location to investment in other sectors or locations.[6] This budgetary process has served to funnel government receipts collected at all levels through the central government, giving Peking allocative control and thus considerable ability to determine the rate and direction of China's economic development. It is likely to continue as an important characteristic of the Chinese economic system.[7]

[5]These profits of state enterprises have accounted for almost nine-tenths of the government's budget revenue in recent years.

[6] For example, investment in Shanghai in 1949–1973 represented only 6.7 percent of the revenue accumulated in Shanghai for the state budget over the same period. See Nicholas Richard Lardy, "Central Control and Redistribution in China: Central-Provincial Fiscal Relations since 1949," unpublished Ph.D. dissertation, The University of Michigan, 1975, p. 202.

[7]There is a debate in the literature concerning the consequences of China's budgetary process and the considerable decentralization that has occurred in the economy since 1957. Some observers believe the effects of decentralized *collection* of budget revenue, revenue sharing, and local control over enterprises has led to the reappearance of "cellular," or regional, autonomy in China. See Audrey Donnithorne, "China's Cellular Economy: Some Economic Trends since the Cultural Revolution," *China Quarterly,* no. 52, pp. 605–619, and several other articles by the same author. I believe that my summary of the

ECONOMIC PERFORMANCE

The Chinese leaders have used this institutional reorganization of the economy to achieve an impressive record of economic development over the past two decades. The most noteworthy, or most readily quantifiable, achievements were obtained in the industrial sector. Inheriting a sector limited in size and considerably distorted in its structural and geographical distribution,[8] Peking allocated to this sector the largest share of investment between 1949 and the mid-1970s. As a result, industrial output increased more than eightyfold during that period, i.e., at an average annual rate of increase of approximately 13 percent or a doubling of the level of output every five years.[9] This remarkable pace of industrialization was

---

opposing view that considerable control is retained by the central government represents the conclusions of most observers.

[8]In the 1930s, China's modern manufacturing and mining enterprises accounted for less than 10 percent of GNP and employed only about 1 percent of the total population. Approximately one-third of these modern enterprises were foreign-owned, most were located in a few major industrial centers on China's eastern seaboard, and most of the output was in the consumer goods industries. Considerable growth of heavy industry occurred during the war years, both under the Nationalist government's direct investment in the interior and under the Japanese during their occupation of Manchuria and the eastern coastal cities. See Yu-kwei Cheng, *Foreign Trade and Industrial Development of China*, The University Press of Washington, D.C., Washington, D.C., 1956. Nevertheless, even in 1952 the modern manufacturing sector still accounted for less than 12 percent of China's Gross Domestic Product (GDP), while the industrial production of consumer goods accounted for three-fourths of total industrial production in 1949. See Dwight Perkins, "Growth and Changing Structure of China's Twentieth-Century Economy," in Dwight Perkins (ed.), *China's Modern Economy in Historical Perspective*, Stanford University Press, Stanford, Calif., 1975, p. 117, and State Statistical Bureau, *Ten Great Years*, Foreign Languages Press, Peking, 1960, p. 90.

[9]To avoid repetitive citations throughout the remainder of this study, unless otherwise noted all statistical data used is from Nai-ruenn Ch'en, *Chinese Economic Statistics: A Handbook for Mainland China*, Aldine, Chicago, 1967; State Statistical Bureau, *Ten Great Years*; and CIA, *People's Republic of China: Handbook of Economic Indicators*, A(ER)75-72, August 1975. Although there is considerable debate over the accuracy of these data, most

interrupted only twice during the last 25 years: once in the early 1960s, when the lack of inputs and demand for outputs due to the serious agricultural crises following the Great Leap Forward resulted in considerable excess capacity in industry, and again in 1967, when the Cultural Revolution spread to the industrial labor force and into the factory itself, disrupting the normal flow of production.

Increases in industrial output can be obtained most readily by the mere accumulation of capital, i.e., by investment. Inefficiency due to an inexperienced labor force is a problem in China, just as it is in any other underdeveloped country. Nonetheless, when the leadership wanted to obtain more output, say of steel, with the available raw materials and supply of labor (even given its relatively low productivity), that output could be obtained by building another iron mine and steel mill. Bottlenecks were bound to occur. Transportation problems, for example, have been critical in China's development, but high rates of industrial growth can be obtained by "buying" them, and the Chinese leadership has had the ability and willingness to pay the price.[10]

First, the centralized budgetary process tapped the profits of all

---

experts now agree that the "official" statistics are not falsified. Furthermore, these data are used as illustrations of general tendencies or relationships, not as accurate point estimates; the use of one set of estimates rather than another should not change my arguments. The general rates of growth for the past two and one-half decades which are presented in this study obviously overstate the normal rates of growth experienced during most of that period because of the use of the abnormally low base figures in 1949. For example, although industrial production increased at an average annual rate of 13 percent between 1949 and 1974, the annual increase was 10.5 percent between 1952 and 1974, or a doubling of the level of output every seven rather than five years. Thus, the growth rate presented is very sensitive to the period to which it refers, and the reader should be similarly sensitive to this qualification.

[10]This is true, of course, of most communist leaders throughout the world, i.e., the willingness and ability to collect and direct investment funds into industry for the purpose of rapid industrialization. Although it is the leadership who has the ability and willingness to collect and direct the investible funds into industry, it must be pointed out that it is the consumers, through the loss of potential consumption and other sectors (such as agriculture and transportation) and through the loss of potential investment, who end up "paying the price."

enterprises and put them in the hands of the state for reinvestment in industry.[11] (Their control over prices and wages allowed the Chinese leadership to ensure that these profits would be large.) Second, in the context of centralized planning the state assumed responsibility for the collection of revenues and the distribution of produced goods, and thus left industrial managers primarily responsible only for increasing output. These managers were freed from the responsibility of increasing sales and profit margins and of always working toward greater efficiency. The centralized planning system determined what would be produced, where, and in what quantity—no matter at what level of government the targets for production were set (national in the 1950s; provincial, municipal, and county in more recent years). The state then allocated resources according to the centralized plan and directed industrial managers to increase output. Whatever the quality of output or the need for that output, the budgetary and planning process in China assures the allocation of resources to create industrial capacity and the use of that capacity to increase output.[12]

Finally, with a relatively small industrial capacity to begin with, especially in the producer goods industries, China would have been unable to attain these rapid rates of growth if it had not secured a source of capital goods (i.e., machinery and equipment from abroad. Again the state's control over the economy—through the rationing of necessities, mobilization of

---

[11]Already in 1958, state budget revenue was one-third of national income, three-fourths of the state's budget revenue came from state enterprises, almost two-thirds of budget expenditures went for economic construction, more than half those funds went to construction in industry, accumulation accounted for almost one-third of national income, and industrial output for over one-fourth of national income.

[12]As shall be apparent below, the failure to use this budgetary process to divert sufficient resources to agriculture and the inability of the planning process to work anywhere near as well as in the agricultural sector with cooperative units of production has led to considerably different results between those two sectors. This feature of traditional socialist priorities and systems of planning sooner or later gives rise to a contradiction—rapid growth rates in industry and failures in agriculture—and a need to change those priorities or to change the system of planning.

commodities for export, and restriction of the use of these export earnings for the purchase of producer goods imports—made this possible.[13] Faced with the Western embargo on shipments of producer goods, Peking found a source of these goods within the socialist bloc, which not only supplied the Chinese with 6.5 billion U.S. dollars worth of machinery and equipment from 1952 through 1973 but also accepted Chinese exports of raw and processed agricultural products, especially textiles, as payment.[14]

Although the socialist bloc supplied almost three-fourths of China's imports of machinery and equipment in 1952–1973, two-thirds of these were sent to China in the 1950s, when the socialist bloc supplied over 90 percent of China's total imports of machinery and equipment. When the open break between China and the Soviet Union occurred in 1960, the Chinese began to look to Western sources for these producer goods. The Western embargo had been steadily eroded after the early 1950s; since 1960 approximately one-half of China's imports of machinery and equipment has been supplied by Western industrial nations, especially Japan.

Of equal importance was the ability of China's leaders to restructure the composition of industry. Heavy industry, or the manufacturing of producer goods, was initially given the highest

[13]Centralized purchase of grain and raw materials in the agricultural sector by state trading agencies was introduced in the early 1950s; rationing of grain and textiles was introduced in the countryside in 1953 and in urban areas in 1955. During the 1950s, raw and processed agricultural products made up approximately three-fourths of China's exports, and imports of machinery and equipment accounted for more than one-third of total imports and more than one-fourth of the total domestic investment in machinery and equipment. In the 1970s, when China's rate of self-sufficiency in machinery and equipment had increased significantly as a result of the development of the machine-building industry in the 1950s and 1960s, imports of machinery and equipment still accounted for almost one-fifth of total imports.

[14]In the 1950s, Chinese imports of producer goods from the socialist bloc were financed, in part, by some short-term commercial credit and long-term loans. But the Chinese had repaid these debts by 1965—a remarkable record for an underdeveloped country engaged in a large-scale program of industrialization.

priority in the pursuit of self-dependency, i.e., the desire to create a domestic supply equal to the needs created by the scheduled rapid increases in output in all sectors of the economy. The development of the machine-building, energy, and metallurgy sectors—the three key producer goods industries— was of key importance in this effort. While the average annual rate of increase in total industrial production was 13 percent in 1949–1973, output in the machine-building industry increased by more than 20 percent annually in that same period. As a result, the rate of self-sufficiency in machinery and equipment increased from approximately 75 percent in the 1950s to more than 90 percent in the 1970s.[15] In 1952, coal was the source of over 95 percent of China's energy supply, two-thirds of which was consumed in the residential/commercial sector.[16] The consumption of energy increased by over 10 percent annually between 1952 and 1974; industry and construction accounted for almost two-thirds of the total consumption by the end of the period. Energy supplied by coal increased only 8 percent annually between 1952 and 1974. Although in 1974 coal still supplied over two-thirds of the energy consumed in China, the 10 percent annual increase in consumption of energy was made possible by the very rapid increase in energy supplied by oil and natural gas, especially in the 1960s and early 1970s. Between 1965 and 1974, energy supplied by petroleum and natural gas, respectively, increased by 20 and 14 percent annually. Finally, the output of iron ore, pig iron, crude steel, and finished steel all increased at an average annual rate of over 20 percent between 1949 and 1974.[17]

[15]Robert F. Dernberger, "Economic Development and Modernization in Contemporary China," Statistical Appendix, forthcoming in *Technology and Communist Culture,* Praeger Publishers, New York. For the period 1952–1973, output in the machine-building sector increased 16 percent annually.

[16]These data and those in the remainder of this paragraph are from CIA, *China: Energy Balance Projections,* A(ER)75-76, November 1975.

[17]For 1952–1974, the average annual increases in output were 15 percent for iron ore, 14 percent for pig iron, 14 percent for crude steel, and 13 percent for finished steel. See Alfred H. Vsack, Jr. and James D. Egan, "China's Iron and Steel Industry," in *China: A Reassessment of the Economy,* A Compendium of Papers Submitted to the Joint Economic Committee, Congress of the United States, U.S. Government Printing Office, Washington, D.C., 1975.

Because of these high rates of growth in the energy, metallurgy, and machine-building sectors, the producer goods industries as a whole increased their share in total industrial production from about 25 percent in 1949 to over 60 percent in 1974. This dramatic change merely reflects the high priority assigned to the producer goods industries, and the lion's share of investment in fixed capital that that sector received compared with the share that went to the consumer goods industries, where output grew at the more modest annual average rate of 11 percent[18] Thus, by taking advantage of the high payoffs of extensive development in the producer goods industries, the Chinese attained very high growth rates over the past quarter-century, which have contributed to a significant increase in the economy's self-sufficiency, significant changes in the structure of the economy, a relatively high growth rate for the economy as a whole, and very creditable rate of growth in GNP per capita.

The very concentration of investment in producer goods that was responsible for the sector's past success led, paradoxically, to seriously disproportionate development both within the industrial sector as a whole and among it and other parts of the economy. Many of these problems emerged rather quickly; in an attempt to cope with them, the Chinese have already been forced to change their initial priorities for the allocation of investment. Yet these problems continue as the most serious the Chinese face in their economic development effort, and they threaten even the three key producer goods industries that they were originally intended to benefit.

For example, China has taken advantage of most of the relatively cheap (i.e., those involving relatively low marginal capital to output ratios) gains of extensive development; further development in the producer goods industries will depend on investment involving much higher marginal capital-to-output ratios. In the machine-building industry, China is now capable of supplying most rural areas with lathes, milling machines, shapers, and grinders for multiple uses. Future increases in output in the

[18]For 1952–1974, the average annual rate of growth of the consumer goods industries was 8 percent.

machine-building industry must concentrate on the provision of precision and complex machine tools, large-scale and heavy-duty machines, and automated machinery. China's industry requires these in order to increase quality control and efficiency, produce a wider range of products, and be able to produce larger items on a continuous basis. In the energy industry, further rapid increases in energy supplies will depend, as they have in the past decade, on China's ability to derive them from high-cost petroleum and hydroelectric power investments. In metallurgy, a serious bottleneck exists in precision-rolling capacity and in the production of quality alloys. In other words, the cost of obtaining further rapid increases in the production of these key producer goods industries has increased significantly between the mid-1950s and today.[19]

Second, the past emphasis on these three key producer goods industries was at the expense of two other producer goods industries—transportation equipment and producer goods for agriculture. Rail is the major source of modern transport in China, but with approximately 50,000 kilometers of track in the 1970s, China's rail network compares rather poorly with that of other large countries.[20] Rail transportation has also been limited by the shortage of locomotives: China produced only 180 locomotives in 1952–1955. The result of these two deficiencies was a very significant increase in traffic density and weight hauled per train. To increase the potential weight load for the rail network and take

[19]The argument concerning the higher cost involved in obtaining further increases in industrial output, both here and in the examples to follow, explicitly includes the need to solve increasingly difficult technological problems.

[20]In 1949, China's rail network "was about equal in length to the United States system of the mid-1850s or the Soviet system of the late 1870s." See Philip W. Vetterlin and James J. Wagy, "China: The Transportation Sector, 1950–71," in *People's Republic of China: An Economic Assessment*, Compendium of Papers Submitted to the Joint Economic Committee, Congress of the United States, Washington, D.C., May, 1972, p. 151. The data on the transport sector in the following paragraphs are also taken from this source. Although construction since 1949 has tried to correct for the locational distortion of the Chinese rail network, by connecting all provinces and regions (except Tibet) to the rail network, one-third of China's rail network was still located in the northeast in the 1970s.

advantage of their ample petroleum resources, the Chinese have begun to produce larger diesel engines. Production of loco-motives remained relatively stable at between 200 and 300 units per year in 1967–1973. Nonetheless, both the stock of diesels and the weight load per train increased during that period.

Motor transport has emerged as a major provider of short-haul transport in China since the beginning of domestic production of trucks in 1956. The highway network covered about 650,000 kilometers by the early 1970s, most of which are natural earth or gravel roads. Not only is the size of this road network relatively small for a country as large as China and its quality very poor, but annual production of trucks is still less than 150,000 units a year. Thus, although China's rapidly growing supplies of petroleum augur well for the development of modern transportation, China still faces considerable problems in increasing the extent and improving the quality of the rail and road network (e.g., double tracking of railroads and paving of roads, as well as increased maintenance) and in significantly increasing the domestic production of transport equipment.[21] Again, these programs will involve relatively expensive investments that do not *directly* contribute to increases in output. They contribute indirectly by providing the necessary "social overhead" capital—which

---

[21]This is not to say that the Chinese have been unable, through intensive use of the existing facilities and equipment, to facilitate the growth of output in the economy which actually occurred; the average annual rate of increase in industrial production of 13 percent over the past 25 years was equal to the rate of growth in tons hauled by the modern transportation services. But modern transportation is a serious constraint at the margin; it can prevent higher growth rates in production and a more rational distribution of what is produced. Although the modern transportation sector did provide the services necessary to attain the rates of growth actually realized in the past, it did so by depending considerably on imports. For example, transportation equipment worth 750 million U.S. dollars was imported from the noncommunist countries in 1961–1973; this total accounts for more than one-third of China's machinery and equipment imports from those countries. During that same period, China im-ported transportation worth over 350 million U.S. dollars from the Soviet Union, which constituted one-half of China's machinery and equipment from that country. See CIA, *Foreign Trade in Machinery and Equipment Since 1952*, A(ER) 75-60, January 1975.

includes capital for the provision of roads, housing, hospitals, communication, banking and trading facilities, other public utilities, etc.—for the efficient operation of a modern economy. In other words, they facilitate increases of production by eliminating the very serious distribution and delivery problems in the supply of inputs to producers. Equally important, they alleviate the serious problem the Chinese still have in distributing processed goods to their users.

One of the most important consequences of the high priority given heavy industries in the allocation of investment was that these investments were made at the expense of investments in agriculture. In the early 1950s, the Chinese recognized this problem but expected most investment in the agricultural sector to be provided by those working the land. Furthermore, Peking hoped to attain increases in agricultural output from increased labor productivity or higher yields without having to rely on significant increases in the capital intensity of farming. As will be argued below, these hopes were unfounded, largely because of the failure of the state to replace the expropriated landlord as a source of credit for the Chinese peasant and because the peasants had pushed the traditional labor-intensive agriculture technology well into the range of diminishing returns. Even if the peasants had been able to achieve a significant rate of savings from their low per capita incomes, however, the allocation of state investment *within* the industrial sector favored the three key heavy industries at the expense of industries producing agricultural machinery and inputs. In the early 1950s, the output of agricultural machinery did increase over fortyfold, reaching a level of more than 2 million units in 1956.[22] But most of this increase occurred in 1956 alone, when production of plows—especially Soviet model 2 and 3 bladed plows, which were later found to be ill-suited for Chinese farming—increased by over 1 million units.

Following the agricultural crises in 1959–1960, industries

[22]The data for the production of agricultural machinery in this paragraph are from CIA, *Production of Machinery and Equipment in the People's Republic of China*, A(ER)75-63, May 1975.

manufacturing producer goods for agriculture, such as agricultural machinery and equipment and chemical fertilizer, were given a much greater priority in the allocation of investment. Between 1961 and 1973, the total horsepower of irrigation equipment increased from 700,000 to 6 million. Thus, by 1973, China is estimated to have had 30 billion horsepower of irrigation and drainage equipment installed and 41 percent of the total arable land irrigated (compared with 31 percent in 1957). Further increases in the amount of irrigated land undoubtedly will be more and more costly. Production of tractors, introduced in 1958, increased from about 13,000 15-horsepower units in 1961 to 138,000 in 1973, while the production of garden (or walking) tractors, introduced in 1964, increased from 150 15-horsepower units in 1964 to 28,000 in 1973. Thus, by 1973, China is estimated to have had an inventory of almost 700,000 tractors (in 15-horsepower units). These tractors help reduce the physical burden of agricultural labor, significantly reduce the amount of time required to finish tasks during the peak seasons, and provide the peasant with a modern means of transportation. In other words, their main contribution has not been to increase yields but to allow for significant savings of labor, thus freeing labor for the wide range of construction work involved in the transformation of Chinese agriculture now under way in the countryside.

The most significant change that has resulted from the greater allocation of investment in the early 1960s to industries producing inputs for the agricultural sector is the very rapid rate of growth in the chemical fertilizer industry. Until 1958, China imported more chemical fertilizer than it produced domestically. It relied primarily, however, on organic fertilizer; the total supply of chemical fertilizer, from both domestic production and imports, was no greater than 3 million tons (standard units) at the end of the 1950s, less than 10 kilograms of chemical nutrient per hectare.[23] Between 1961 and 1974, the production of chemical fertilizer increased by over 20 percent annually. The domestic

[23]The data for chemical fertilizer production, imports, and supplies in this paragraph are from CIA, *People's Republic of China: Chemical Fertilizer Supplies, 1949–1974*, A(ER)75-70, August 1975.

supply of chemical fertilizer, however, is still woefully inadequate for China's needs; scarce holdings of foreign exchange have been used to import approximately 7 million tons of chemical fertilizer annually over the past 8 years. In addition, 26 chemical fertilizer plants were purchased abroad between November 1972 and May 1974. When operating at full capacity, these plants will add more than 3.5 million tons to the production of nitrogen, which is more than China's total production in 1974.

Although the change in priorities in the 1960s has already done much to offset the earlier neglect of industries producing inputs for agriculture, China's needs for irrigation and drainage equipment, agricultural machinery and equipment, and chemical fertilizer still far exceed its domestic supplies. The continued rapid expansion of these industries is a necessary condition, as it has been for the past decade and a half, for solving China's agricultural problem. As shall be evident below, increases in the output of these industrial products are relatively costly, especially in the fertilizer industry; even were China to meet that cost, the increased supply of these industrially produced inputs for agriculture can be expected—on the basis of both historical evidence and economic theory—to obtain declining increases in agricultural production as the irrigated acreage, level of mechanization, and use of chemical fertilizer are expanded.

The relative neglect of investment in the transportation sector and, until recently, in producer goods for the agricultural sector has served to limit the access of rural areas to the products of modern industry. One of the ramifications of this neglect is the need to restructure the geographical location of industry. For example, industries in Peking, Tientsin, and Shanghai—three cities with significant social overhead capital and trained industrial workers—accounted for 27 percent of total industrial output in both 1952 and 1973.[24] The Chinese are attempting to redress the traditional geographical concentration of industrial activity in their country. They have attempted to control the

[24]Charles Robert Roll, Jr., and Kung-chia Yeh, "Balance in Coastal and Inland Industrial Development," in *China: A Reassessment of the Economy*, p. 88.

traditional pattern of urbanization and shift in shares of the labor force from agriculture to industry which is usually associated with modernization by fostering small-scale industrial production units in the countryside, not allowing the indiscriminate migration of rural labor to the cities, and actually reversing the traditional flow by sending educated youths to work in the countryside after they complete high school.[25] Although large-scale modern industry may retain its share of total industrial output, the development of new industries in the rural areas is fostering a new type of urbanization in China—the rapid growth of medium-size cities. The growth of new industrial centers is also fostered by the growth of the new petroleum industry. (Only 13 percent of China's crude oil was produced in the coastal provinces in 1970.) Although this redistribution of industrial activity will serve to reduce the demands on China's transportation network, it will also greatly increase the investment of capital for social overhead expenses required in these newly emerging medium-size cities in the rural areas. Furthermore, not only is the rural labor force less experienced in industrial production and thus less productive than is the labor force in the traditional urban and coastal industrial centers, but it also produces lower-quality goods.

Finally, the unbalanced growth within industry has added to the constraints on raising per capita consumption at the expense of investment. The significant increase in GNP per capita since 1949 is not indicative of an equivalent increase in consumption per capita. The Chinese leadership's control over employment in industry, wage increases, and prices of consumer goods enable them to control the effective demand for consumer goods.[26] The desire to maintain lower prices for necessities requires the use of

[25]A major reason, of course, for developing these medium-size industrial centers and rural industries in the countryside is not the purely economic considerations of costs and benefits but the Chinese leadership's desire to break down the traditional social divisions between rural and urban dwellers and to avoid the social problems traditionally associated with very large urban concentrations of population.

[26]See Dwight Perkins, *Market Control and Planning in Communist China*, Harvard University Press, Cambridge, Mass., 1966, especially chapters VIII and IX.

rationing to assure the equitable distribution of a relatively scarce supply. Prices of industrially produced consumer durables (e.g., bicycles, watches, sewing machines, radios, etc.) are set relatively high. Nonetheless, to provide consumer goods to workers the Chinese Communists increased investment in consumer goods industrial production in the 1960s and 1970s and—to maintain incentives—must continue this policy in the future.

Although detailed statistics are not available, several bits of evidence can be cited in support of an argument that increases in the standard of living have not been very significant since the mid-1950s, especially in light of China's overall rate of growth. Grain supplies per capita have not increased significantly, and domestic consumption has been maintained by large-scale imports during the past decade. Basic foodstuffs and cotton cloth continue to be rationed, and the rations per capita have not increased significantly. Increases in wages are obtained by moving up the existing grade-scale, but the wages for each grade in industry have remained relatively stable. The most important means for increasing household income in China is the move from agriculture into industry or from a relatively low-wage industry to a relatively high-wage industry, but these moves are strictly controlled and limited. These constraints on increases in personal income are somewhat offset by the increased provision of public goods and services, such as health and heavily subsidized education and housing. Nonetheless, these goods and services are much more available to the urban industrial workers, a very small portion of the total labor force, than to those living in the rural areas.

Any visitor to China can attest to the fact that the average Chinese enjoys a decent standard of living; deviations from the average are strikingly limited. Furthermore, the household is the consuming unit in China; given the young population and a very high rate of participation in the labor force, consumption per household has probably increased more than statistics on consumption per capita would indicate. Sample surveys for the mid-1950s showed that the national average per capita consumption was approximately 250 kilograms of food grains, 6 to 8 meters of cotton cloth, 10 kilograms of pork, and 125 kilograms of vegetables. These items accounted for over 50 percent of the consumer's budget. Since the 1950s, the supplies of vegetables and manufactured consumer goods such as shoes and synthetic fiber textiles have increased, but it is unlikely that the average annual increase in total consumption per capita has averaged much more than 1 percent annually over the past 20 years, a total increase of about 25 percent.

The only way that the Chinese labor force would enjoy a larger share of the fruits of China's industrial development is if industrial production of consumer goods—such as clothing, household goods, watches, bicycles, radios, sewing machines, and even cameras (the last five items being obvious indicators of higher standards of living in China today)—were increased. The obstacle here, however, is not just the allocation of a greater percentage of investment to these industries. Many of these industries, which rely heavily on inputs of agricultural products, have experienced periods of excess capacity over the past quarter-century due to the slow rate of growth of agricultural production. In other words, the rapid development of the consumer goods industries, as well as the rapid growth of the standard of living in China, depends on the rapid growth of agricultural production—the greatest bottleneck in China's economic development.

The agricultural sector suffered most from the Chinese leadership's past allocation of the largest share of investment to the producer goods industrial sector. As mentioned earlier, the investment funds accumulated in the budget were considered to be for state-owned and -operated projects (i.e., industry), while the cooperative sector was expected to be responsible for the accumulation of its own investment funds. For example, only 7.6 percent of the investment in capital construction in the First Five Year Plan was scheduled for agriculture; most of these funds were used for large-scale water conservation projects. Additional funds were allocated for the reclamation of wasteland by military units and for rural relief. The peasants themselves were called upon to provide an amount three times the state's investment, with the state providing agricultural loans equal to only 15 percent of planned peasant savings and investments.[27] Estimates indicate that less than one-fifth of the sales of commodities in the rural sector in 1953–1956 were of producer goods. Almost half of these consisted of inputs used up in current production, i.e., fertilizer and traditional farm implements; only about 5 percent of these commodities, or less than 1 percent of the total commodities sold to the rural areas, consisted of modern farm implements and irrigation equipment.[28]

The consequences of placing a priority on developing heavy industry as a prerequisite for developing other industries were understood by the Chinese leadership. They recognized that this policy implied a considerable lag before Chinese agriculture could be supplied with industrially produced producer goods for use in obtaining increases in agricultural production. The leadership was divided, however, between those, such as Liu Shao-ch'i, who argued that agriculture production could be socialized into large-scale cooperatives only after it was mechanized (i.e., modernized), and those, such as Mao Tse-tung, who argued that socialization of the relations of production should precede mechanization or modernization. The Maoists won this debate in the mid-1950s.

The socialization of agriculture, however, was not advocated by the Maoists solely on the basis of the desirable social and political effects it would have on the peasantry. Along with socialists elsewhere, the Maoists believed that the creation of ever larger cooperative units of production would "unleash" the production powers of the peasants; these peasants, through their cooperative labor efforts, would then provide for increases in output that would be large enough to meet the demands of the nonagricultural parts of the economy and provide for an increase in the peasants' standard of living as well. In other words, the Maoists believed that even in the absence of large-scale investments or industrially produced modern inputs, this

[27]Data from *First Five-Year Plan for the Development of the National Economy of the People's Republic of China in 1953–1957*, Foreign Language Press, Peking, 1956.

[28]Shigeru Ishikawa, *National Income and Capital Formation in Mainland China*, Institute of Asian Economic Affairs, Tokyo, 1965, pp. 177–179.

institutional reorganization of agricultural production alone would solve China's agricultural problem in the short run; the modernization of agriculture could come later as a trickle-down effect of industrialization.

It was not long, however, before the inevitable short-run contradictions of this development strategy became evident. In the early 1950s, the restoration of peace and stability; the rational pooling of land, labor, and capital in the *early* stages of the collectivization movement; and good weather allowed for increases in both the *level* of output and in the *share* of that output transferred to the state. But increases in the gross value of agricultural output, which averaged 14 percent annually in 1949–1952, slowed down to a rate of only 5 percent annually in 1952–1957. The average annual rate of increase for *grain* output in 1952–1957 was 3.7 percent, which was close to the target as revised downward in the First Five Year Plan. This increase in total grain production was largely achieved by giving high-yield grain crops (rice and potatoes) priority at the expense of wheat and oil crops, which failed to achieve their targets. Most important, once the state's share of grain output had increased in 1953 to the approximate level of the share of output sold by the producer in the prewar period and rationing had been introduced, the annual net supply of grain available to the state remained relatively constant in the period 1956–1957.[29] This situation severely limited the state's ability to supply food for the urban areas (which was necessary if it was to increase the industrial labor force), to obtain the raw materials in order to increase industrial production of consumer goods, and to increase exports of agricultural products in order to finance imports required to provide for increases in investment and heavy industrial production. These constraints are reflected in various economic indicators for 1957: a decline of employment in the nonagricultural sector, an increase of only 5.6 percent in the industrial production of consumer goods, a decrease in exports,

[29]David Ladd Denny, "Rural Policies and the Distribution of Agricultural Products in China: 1950–1959," unpublished Ph.D. dissertation, University of Michigan, 1971, p. 41.

and a decline in total capital construction. In fact, the rate of growth for the economy as a whole in 1957 was the lowest of any year since the establishment of the PRC in 1949.

Despite the lack of any empirical evidence to show an increase in output associated with the socialization of agriculture, the Chinese decided to launch the Great Leap Forward and the commune movement in 1958. They thought that this attempt to make an immediate transition to the advanced stage of socialism in agricultural production, rather than a reallocation of the state's investments or a change in its priorities for development, would solve their agricultural problem. Very favorable weather, the best in the Far East for several decades, and a tremendous increase in the labor force boosted grain output by 19 percent and the gross value of agricultural output by 25 percent in 1958. Bad weather in 1959 and the delayed harmful effects of the attempt to introduce such a large-scale and advanced socialist organization into traditional Chinese agriculture, however, resulted in a serious agricultural crisis in 1959–1961. The level of grain output was not restored to the peak level of 1958 until 1965.

This severe crisis forced the Chinese to reevaluate their development strategy and to recognize the need to solve the agricultural problem by changing their allocation strategies and priorities for development. Most of the resulting policy changes have been mentioned earlier: the reestablishment of the team or the brigade as the effective locus of decision making for agricultural production and distribution; an increase in industrial production of producer goods for agriculture, especially agricultural machinery and equipment (tractors, irrigation equipment, transplanters, harvesters, threshers, etc.), chemical fertilizers, and cement (for farmland reconstruction and irrigation projects); the creation of small-scale industries in the rural areas to manufacture these producer goods; and an acceleration of the rate at which the supply of these goods could be increased, among others. A more extensive description of China's attempt to solve its agricultural problem and the likelihood of its success will follow in Chapter Four. Nonetheless, it can be noted here that the results obtained thus far have not been very striking. Between 1964 and 1974, the average annual rate of increase in grain output was less than 3 percent; China had to rely on sizable grain imports to make up for the deficits in domestic supply. Agricultural development remains the major constraint to overall economic development and increases in the standard of living.

This review of the past performance and current state of the Chinese economy has not attempted to provide a complete or detailed description of China's economy over the past quarter-century. Rather, its purpose has been to show how the Chinese Communists gained control over the allocation of resources and how they used that control to achieve rapid increases in heavy industrial production, a relatively high overall rate of growth, and a significant restructuring of the economy. This mechanism for control is likely to be retained at least for the next few decades. Yet the successful record of the Chinese is qualified by their failure to follow a more balanced sense of priorities, which has resulted in serious bottlenecks to future growth in transportation, consumption, and agriculture.[30]

None of the preceding discussion is intended to imply that China's pursuit of the traditional socialist development priorities in the allocation of investment was unwise. While the Chinese have not solved all the problems of economic development, they have created a substantial industrial base and have been able to provide their people an adequate standard of living for the past 25 years. It is on the basis of this review of China's past record that this essay turns to an analysis of the probability of Chinese success in the decades ahead. The next section discusses two major aspects of China's economic environment that can be assumed to remain fixed in the near future.

[30]This successful record of growth must be qualified by the instability that marked that record, as noted in Chapter One. One set of estimates for China's economic growth over the last quarter-century (1949–1974) yields a cumulative average annual rate of growth of 7.1 percent. (Estimates from CIA, A(ER) 75-72, *People's Republic of China: Handbook of Economic Indicators*, August 1975). Yet if we look at the actual annual rates of growth for the 25 individual years within this period, only 1 year of the last 17 had a rate of growth between 6 and 8 percent. For the period as a whole, four annual rates of growth were negative, four were between 0 and 6 percent, four between 6 and 8 percent, five between 8 and 12 percent, five between 12 and 15 percent, and three greater than 15 percent.

THREE

The Fixed Parameters

There is probably no dimension of China's social or political situation that can safely be assumed as fixed. Nonetheless, several characteristics of that situation are likely to remain relatively stable over the next 10 to 15 years, because the Chinese decision makers will be either unable to change them or unlikely to want to do so. The most important of these concern China's resource base and its economic and political system.

THE RESOURCE BASE

As was argued in Chapter Two, the most fundamental obstacle to economic development in China is the need to solve the agricultural problem. Yet the very deficiencies in agriculture that led to the development problems do not themselves seem readily amenable. The search for a solution must take as "relatively fixed" the available area of cultivated land, its location, its fertility, and the existing climatic conditions. More than one-half of China's land mass is over 2,000 meters above sea level. Only about 15 percent of China's total acreage is considered suitable for agriculture. Since fertile land is scarce and confined to five major regions—the Manchurian plain, the North China plain, the Yangtze River valley and delta, the Pearl River delta, and the Szechwan Basin—over the past 40 centuries China's farmers have settled that land and brought most of the available fertile acreage under cultivation. Cultivated acreage is estimated to have expanded less than 0.5 percent annually between 1400 and 1957.[1] The richest agricultural soil is found on the North China plain, and the quality progressively deteriorates toward the South; in South China, the soil is leached and poor in humus. Yet, because of climatic conditions—abundant and dependable rainfall in the south and insufficient and undependable rainfall in the North—the actual productivity of these cultivated areas is highest in the southern regions and lowest in the northern areas. Thus, the highest population densities are found in the Pearl River delta (near Canton) and the Szechwan Basin, the lowest on the Manchurian plain.

Nonetheless, the Chinese peasants have been able to support almost one-fourth of the world's population with less than 8 percent of the world's cultivated area by means of a relatively traditional labor-intensive technology. The problem the Chinese face, of course, is the need to achieve a significant and steady rate of increase in productivity on this limited cultivated area, which in turn is subject to unfavorable soil and climate conditions. While the Chinese may be able to achieve some increases in cultivated area, the necessary increases in agricultural output cannot come from a new lands policy. Equally important, in terms of China's role in the future international system, the annexation of the lands adjacent to China's borders would not provide the solution to this problem. Rather, the increases must come from the spread of double cropping and irrigation, the increased use of chemical fertilizer, changes in the cropping pattern, the use of new seeds, etc. This agricultural transformation is being sought through the current programs of significant technological change and intensive, rather than extensive, investment. The success of these programs is crucial to China's economic development.

Yet agricultural transformation is only a necessary, not a sufficient, condition for modernization. Therefore the Chinese are also pursuing the rapid development of industry. To become an industrial giant, a country must have access to raw materials. Given the urgency of China's industrialization program, Peking's

---

[1] Dwight Perkins, *Agricultural Development in China, 1368–1968*, Aldine, Chicago, 1969, p. 16.

desire to create a domestic production capacity in the entire range of industries, and the limited export capacity of the economy (due to limited supply and large demand domestically), the success of China's industrial program depends to a considerable extent on China's domestic resource base. The length of this paper precludes an extensive discussion of this base, but two critical categories of raw materials for modern industry can be evaluated briefly—namely, energy sources and minerals. China is quite richly endowed in both.[2]

In terms of energy resources, China is among the first rank in coal, having high-quality, easily mined, and well-distributed reserves. China is the world's second largest producer of anthracite, third largest of bituminous, and fifth largest of coke. China also has an extensive river system, with the third largest water runoff in the world. Although these rivers descend from their mountain sources through narrow valleys and gorges with hard rock formations, allowing for the development of considerable hydroelectric power capacity with relatively small construction costs, 72 percent of the hydro power potential—determined by the rivers' volume, stability, and rate of flow—is located in the Southwest of China at a considerable distance from the centers of industry. In addition, silting problems and irregular flows present serious obstacles to the utilization of China's rivers for power generation. Thus, given China's abundant and widespread coal deposits, over two-thirds of China's electric power is generated in thermal electric power stations.

The ratio between growth in GNP and energy requirements ("energy-GNP elasticity") is between 1 and 2 for most countries; for China this means that a 1 percent increase in GNP will require an increase of between 1 and 2 percent in energy supplies. Therefore, despite the very favorable endowment in coal and river system and the considerable potential for growth that these provide, the solution to China's energy problems is to be found in the exploitation of petroleum deposits. As recently as the mid-1960s,

[2]K. P. Wang, "The Mineral Resource Base of Communist China," in *An Economic Profile of Mainland China*, Studies Prepared for the Joint Economic Committee, Congress of the United States, U.S. Government Printing Office, Washington, D.C., 1967, vol. 1, p. 169.

a review of China's electrical energy resources noted that the hydroelectric and coal resources compared favorably to those in the United States and Soviet Union. It also noted, however, that China's oil resources did not.[3] Proven reserves of natural petroleum were then set at 2 billion tons (15 billion barrels). Remarkable developments over the past 10 years, however, have significantly changed that pessimistic outlook to one of extreme optimism. China's onshore deposits are now believed to be as large as 20 billion barrels, with additional deposits offshore of 30 billion barrels of recoverable oil and 20 billion barrels that can be extracted from shale deposits.[4] Although neither the conversion of industrial facilities from coal-burning to oil-burning nor the exploitation of the petroleum deposits is cheap, China should be able to avoid a serious energy bottleneck in its industrialization program over the next 10 to 15 years by utilizing its own resources.[5]

Nor does a lack of minerals seem likely to impede that program: China has large reserves of all but a few. For instance, there are large surplusses of antimony, mercury, molybdenum, tin, tungsten, and fluorspar and smaller ones of lead, manganese, zinc, asbestos, bauxite, the raw materials for cement, magnesite, salt, sulfur, and talc. China also has adequate deposits of aluminum, iron ore (spread widely throughout the country), graphite, and gypsum. The quality of the iron ore varies significantly but poses no serious technological problem. The most serious scarcities are of chromite (which is obtained from Albania), copper (aluminum is currently substituted for copper in electrical uses), nickel

[3]John Ashton, "Development of Electric Energy Resources in Communist China," in *An Economic Profile*, pp. 297–316.

[4]These estimates are undoubtedly subject to wide margins of error but are being modified as one new deposit after another is discovered. Furthermore, although supported by estimates of Soviet geologists, they are conservative when compared with many Japanese and American estimates. See Selig S. Harrison, "Time Bomb in Asia," *Foreign Policy*, no. 20, Fall 1975. According to Harrison, "Peking appears likely to reach the current production level of Saudi Arabia by 1988 or soon thereafter." Ibid, p. 4.

[5] For an interesting, but somewhat mechanical, projection of future energy demand and supply in China, see CIA, *China: Energy Balance Projections*, A(ER)75-75, November 1975.

(which is obtained through imports), and phosphate rock (which is important for fertilizer production).

This very favorable endowment of resources, especially in these two important categories, means that China's industrialization and drive for self-sufficiency will not likely suffer from serious constraints of raw-material resources. Rather, the major problem facing China's industrialization program concerns the need to accumulate producer goods for the processing of these resources. This need will have important implications not only for China's foreign trade but also for China's role in the international system.[6]

It is not necessary to be a Marxist or a Maoist to realize that China's richest resource is the Chinese people, the largest labor force in the world. Arguments that "surplus" population is a problem in economic development often overlook the importance of labor as an element in any production activity. In fact, this "surplus" population often is working, even if some people are engaged in activities with very low or even zero productivity— "disguised unemployment." Because of the lack of capital for alternative productive activities, however, these people form a burden on the economy in their role as consumers.

[6]In this regard, China does suffer from a shortage of gold and silver, the major commodity reserve assets used in foreign trade. Not being a major producer of these precious metals, the Chinese are unable to maintain sizable import deficits for considerable lengths of time *without* relying on foreign loans. This can have, and has had, serious implications for China's economic development program and foreign trade behavior when an unwillingness to borrow abroad, coupled with a decline or lack of growth in export capacity, leads to a serious constraint on imports. The rapid development of petroleum production has helped to alleviate this constraint on China's development program, but it has not eliminated it.

Another raw material that directly affects China's role in the international system is uranium. China's three uranium mines are reported to be capable of producing 2,500 tons of ore daily, which is enough to support China's modest program for developing a nuclear weapon system. In fact, not all the uranium produced has been used domestically; some of the processed uranium has been exchanged with the Czechs for the latter's help in building the necessary uranium benefication and processing facilities in China. See K. P. Wang, "Natural Resources and Their Utilization," in Yuan-li Wu (ed.), *China: A Handbook,* Praeger Publishers, Inc., New York, 1973, p. 77.

Whatever the merit of this argument against "surplus" population may be in other contexts, it does not apply in China today. As studies for the 1930s and 1940s and the experience of the 1950s have all shown, the combination of labor-intensive agricultural techniques and the concentration of labor required during the peak periods of agricultural production leads to serious labor shortages in rural areas during these peak periods.[7] Furthermore, because of the scale and pace of construction and other nonagricultural activities in the rural areas during the past quarter-century, the demands on the available labor force can even be described as a situation of "overfull employment." There should be no need to argue that China's labor force is able and hard-working: the achievement of remarkably high yields by means of a traditional labor-intensive technology in agriculture offers ample evidence.[8]

China's population over the next 10 to 15 years safely can be assumed as given, even though estimates of its absolute size may be subject to wide margins of error. Currently estimated to be between 800 and 900 million, the population should reach the 1 billion level sometime during the 1980s. While this labor supply is one of China's most valuable resources, the current Chinese efforts to reduce the birthrate seem to contradict its importance. This is because further productivity achieved through increased employment within the traditional labor-intensive technology has already reached the area of diminishing returns and relatively low marginal gains. Instead, China's successful economic evolution depends on modernization, where rapid and steady increases in the productivity of each unit of labor are accomplished essentially by two means: first, the introduction of modern capital-intensive

[7] I am referring to the studies of John Lossing Buck for the 1930s, those of T. H. Shen for the 1940s, and the severe labor shortage the Chinese encountered during the Great Leap Forward.

[8] Visitors to China are struck by the much less hectic nature of production activities in China than prevails in the West, not only in industry, but also in agriculture; machines do not set the pace, laborers do. This is offset, of course, by the fact that more laborers are employed and for longer durations. In addition, the pace quickens significantly when tasks *must* be performed quickly, as in modern industry and during seasonal peak activities.

technology; second, the accumulation of larger amounts of capital for each worker to work with.

During the transition period from traditional labor-intensive to modernized capital-intensive technology, however, a tremendous increase in labor effort will be required, primarily in the countryside. The adoption of a capital-intensive technology in the modern industrialized sector would not only maximize output obtained per unit of investment and per worker but would also free people to work in the countryside. Thus, the present programs to reduce the birthrate and to limit migration to the urban areas, even to the point of forcing a reverse flow, are rational ones in light of the short-run changes and long-run goals involved in the attempt to modernize China's economy. These policies undoubtedly will continue to be implemented during the next 10 to 15 years.

One serious problem that China's large population will certainly present during the next 10 to 15 years involves the precarious balance between the supply and demand for foodstuffs. There is currently a very small margin—if any—between increases in agricultural productivity and the rate of population growth. China's ability to increase this productivity over the next 10 to 15 years will be evaluated in a subsequent section of this essay, but its ability to limit the rate of population growth will be discussed here because I believe it can be considered as a given.

The Chinese have reported remarkable achievements in limiting population growth. Visitors are often given data on birthrates and population growth that are hard to believe: they indicate rates of population growth much lower than those of other underdeveloped countries.[9] In fact, China's data are

[9]Birth and death rates (and total population) are not systematically reported by the Chinese, yet visitors are given very precise data for the particular place they are visiting. Almost all these rates show a net rate of population growth significantly less than 1 percent. A well-known demographer, Professor Ronald Freedman, used the birth and death rates he was given during his trip to China to estimate the demographic profile of the population consistent with those rates. He concluded in an unpublished paper that the implied age-specific fertility rates were unique for countries at similar levels of development. For further evidence of the unreliability of these birth and death rates, see footnote 11, p. 118.

roughly equivalent to those of the highly industrialized (and urbanized) nations. While I do not question the involvement of the people in China's birth control program or its sincerity and broad scope, the data being released are either for a "selected" sample, or they include the net effect of emigration, or they are simply targets that the Chinese hope to achieve. It is difficult to accept these data as indicating the average rate of growth of population for the country as a whole.

Many scholars, on the other hand, estimate a current rate of growth for China's population slightly below 2 percent and expect it to decline to about 1.5 percent by the end of the century.[10] Nonetheless, "Chinese leaders and Chinese publications refer almost consistently to the nice round figure of 2 percent as the growth rate, at best prefacing it with the word 'approximately.' "[11] Actually, whether we accept either 2 or 1.7 percent as the rate of population growth makes little difference for the purposes of this analysis; if the Chinese are unable to increase agricultural production—including not simply food but other agricultural raw materials as well—at a steady annual rate of increase greater than 2 percent, their development program will encounter serious problems. Although the constraints on China's economic development program caused by slow growth in agricultural production were somewhat alleviated by both the state's ability to gain greater control over the allocation of the slow-growing output and its use of imports, the relatively slow agricultural growth led to rationing, very slow growth in the standard of living, periodic but significant excess capacity in light industry, imports of foodstuffs to feed the urban population, and severe constraints

[10]See, for example, the population rates of growth presented in Georges Tapinos, "The World in the 1980s: Demographic Perspectives" (tr. Edward L. Morse), forthcoming in a volume of the 1980s Project.

[11]Leo Orleans, "China's Population: Can the Contradiction Be Resolved?" in *China: A Reassessment of the Economy*, p. 72. When questioned about the Chinese reports of exceptionally low birth- and growth rates by Orleans, the "responsible person" in the Ministry of Health claimed that the State Statistical Bureau, which is responsible for vital rates, was still in a state of flux (following the shake-ups during the Cultural Revolution in the 1960s) and that figures for the "national" birth and death rates "are still not available in China." Ibid.

on China's import capacity due to periodic shortfalls in exports. Whether the rate will be 2 or 1.7 percent over the next 10 to 15 years, in the short run the Chinese still need to increase the standard of living, provide agricultural products for use as inputs for industry and food and clothing for the nonagricultural labor force, and provide exports to pay for the producer goods needed for the development program.[12] The ability of the Chinese to obtain significant increases in yields in agriculture over the next 10 to 15 years will be discussed in Chapter Four.

THE POLITICAL-ECONOMIC SYSTEM

Whatever the results of efforts in the agricultural sector, the broader issue of the stability of China's socialist revolution, which is explicitly assumed in my analysis of the future evolution of China's economy, must be discussed in more detail if the political-economic system is to be adequately understood. Some readers may regard my explicit linkage of fundamental changes in political and economic policies, especially those regarding China's international relations, with the success or failure of China's economic development program as a sort of economic determinism. It is quite the contrary: one of the major tasks of this essay is to identify and suggest the probable outcome of the interaction between politics and economics that is a major feature of both China's economy and its international relations.

There are a number of reasons for arguing that there will be no major revolution in China's political-economic system due to *economic* causes. First, the history of the past quarter-century has provided sufficient testimony of the ability of Chinese leaders to feed their people and to assure them of at least a minimum

[12]Exports of raw and processed agricultural products were 74.9 percent of total exports in 1928 (the peak year of China's pre-1949 foreign trade), 73.2 percent in 1953–1960, and 63.7 percent in 1971–1973. Robert F. Dernberger, "Foreign Trade and Capital Movements of Communist China, 1949–1962," unpublished Ph.D. dissertation, Harvard University, 1965, p. 148; and CIA, *People's Republic of China: International Trade Handbook*, A(ER)74-63, September 1974, p. 12.

standard of living. The problem of maintaining this standard of living, although still present, is much less severe now than it was in the 1950s.[13] Fulfilling this need to maintain an adequate standard of living is obviously a major objective of the Chinese, who have shown their willingness to adopt new and different policies rather quickly when necessary to achieve it. It is unlikely that their development efforts will result in drastic failure, leading to famine, chaos, and counterrevolution.

Second, anticipated grain outputs over the next 10 to 15 years range between low or no growth (0–1 percent) and high rates of growth (3–4 percent).[14] The lowest range appears to be of crisis dimensions. It would yield an output of grain in 1990 that was 67 million tons smaller than that yielded by a 2 percent rate of growth, which is approximately a constant output per capita. In contrast, the output of grain in 1990 would be 83 million tons larger with the high rate than with the 2 percent rate. Thus, the difference between the extremes of this range is 150 million tons—the equivalent of China's total grain output in 1952. Yet none of the range of probable results within these bounds is likely to produce a major change in China's political-economic system. Nonetheless, the lower bound implies relative failure and the higher bound, relative success in China's economic development program—and these different results would likely lead to significant differences in China's role in the international system.

Although revolutionary changes in China's political and economic system are unlikely to result from economic causes, there remains the question of whether conflicts within the

[13]Comparing 1971–1974 with 1953–1957, grain production is approximately 45 percent higher while population is approximately 35 percent higher. China's export capacity has increased more than fourfold over the same period, and China imported an average of 5.6 million tons of grain in the 1971–1974 period compared with none in the earlier period.

[14]A rate of growth of agricultural output of 4 percent would imply a doubling of the level of output in 17½ years. The annual average rate of growth in the gross value of farm output, in constant dollars, in the United States was 3 percent in both the first and second halves of the nineteenth century. This growth, however, was obtained while bringing new lands under cultivation and does not reflect a 3 percent annual increase in yields.

120

leadership may be a source of such changes during the next 10 to 15 years, especially following the recent death of Mao. While any forecasts regarding the leadership are hazardous, the possibility of a take-over by the radical left would seem much more possible than the restoration of capitalism. In fact, I believe the possibility of a "capitalist restoration" in the near future does not exist and will assume this to be the case. The struggle between "moderates" and "radicals," however, is real and likely to continue, which means that economic policies over the next 10 to 15 years may vary between moderation and radicalism.

Although these terms lack precision and are used here as labels for a rather complex grouping of both individuals and policies, they can usefully distinguish between two rough groupings of economic policy options. On the one hand, the moderates give greater priority to economic development as the short-run goal and as a prerequisite for achieving a social transformation. As a result, they place greater emphasis on the more traditional economic policies associated with "efficiency," a rational division of labor, advanced technology and modern industry, and reliance on technicians and engineers. In other words, they favor placing "economics" in command in the short run and leaving the achievement of the goal of social transformation to the long run. Thus, the major constraint on the moderates' program is their short-run challenge to the ideological goals of Mao's socialist revolution.

The radicals, on the other hand, using the Soviet experiences as an example, realize that the moderates' economic policies may well involve the creation and entrenchment in Chinese society of social values and behavior that are antagonistic to the objectives of achieving a true socialist society—so much so that this objective is not only postponed but eventually eliminated. Thus, they see the necessity of simultaneous economic development *and* social transformation. As a result, their economic policies involve a much greater trade-off between the objectives of economic development and social transformation than do those of the moderates. The major constraint on the radicals is therefore the reality of Chinese society today: beset by economic problems and (again, without Mao) with an economic, political, and military system that is disinclined—because of these economic problems—to accept or support them.

At times during the past 25 years, the radicals' impatience in achieving social transformation or reaction to the revisionist implications of the moderates' economic policies led to their implementation of policies that involved considerable trade-offs between the objectives of social transformation and economic development, with a very unfavorable result in terms of economic growth. Because of this experience, the radicals now realize that the socialist transformation is a long-run process that progresses in stages, each advance in the transformation being made possible by increases in the productive capacity of the economy (i.e., the generation of sufficient surplus to allow for a trade-off between economic growth and the desired social transformation) as well as changes in the attitudes and receptiveness of the masses. The latter constraint requires continuous socialist education campaigns to overcome the more "natural" antisocialist values and behavior of human beings and the "capitalist" behavioral values reinforced by the moderates' economic policies. The former constraint requires continuous economic development and, therefore, is a strong force for the continuance of compromise leadership—a real example of the Marxian dialectic.

The policy differences summarized above are largely a matter of emphasis or degree, not contradictory alternatives. Neither group questions the basic political and economic organization of Chinese social institutions that has evolved since 1949. It is this basic set of institutions and policies that can be taken as given in the analyses of developments over the near future.

Nonetheless, this stability regarding institutions and policies means in practice the control of allocative and other economic decisions by central authorities. Whatever group is in power will thereby have both the means to implement the particular policies it advocates and considerable power over the allocation of resources in China. Thus, the composition of China's political leadership over the next 10 to 15 years will naturally affect the probable results of China's struggle with the agricultural problem, the pace and structure of its industrial development program, and the role played by foreign trade (and possibly capital movements) in that program. And the nature of Chinese leadership will of course have important effects on China's role in the international system.

FOUR

The Future Evolution of China's Economy

In his January 1975 "Report on the Work of the Government" to the fourth National People's Congress (NPC) of the PRC, Premier Chou En-lai, referring to Mao's blueprint for the two-stage development of China's economy—the creation of an independent and comprehensive industry by 1980 and the comprehensive modernization of agriculture by the end of the century—said that the next 10 years were crucial for its accomplishment and directed the State Council to "draw up a long-range ten-year plan, five-year plans, and annual plans."[1] According to one observer, the reduction in the number of economic ministries from 40 to 26 announced at the Fourth NPC and the ensuing campaign to impose "the dictatorship of the proletariat" were for the purposes of tightening up the centralized planning and management of the economy and providing for the discipline necessary for the orderly pursuit of these economic development goals over the next decade.[2] No details of these plans have been released, but the most fundamental economic problem faced by the Chinese in their attempt to join the ranks of the industrialized nations remains that of achieving a sustained rate of growth in agricultural production well above their rate of

[1]Chou En-lai, "Report on the Work of the Government," *Peking Review*, no. 4, January 24, 1975, p. 23.

[2]Robert Michael Field, "Civilian Industrial Development in the People's Republic of China: 1949–1974," in *China: A Reassessment of the Economy*, p. 159.

population growth. This problem basically can be reduced to a simple question of the production possibilities in the agrarian sector. *The single most important determinant of China's economic future over the next 15 years will be the ability to increase agricultural production more than 2 percent annually.* The failure to achieve an annual rate of growth exceeding 2 percent would mean the continuation of serious constraints on China's ability to maintain sustained economic growth and to obtain higher standards of living for its people.

AGRICULTURE

Even though the Chinese leadership now recognize the agricultural problem as the prime obstacle to the economic development of China and assigns its alleviation the highest priority in their development programs, the achievement of an average rate of growth in agricultural production of over 2 percent will not be easy. For example, in his study of agricultural development in China over the past six centuries, Dwight Perkins estimates that China's grain output increased yearly by less than 0.5 percent between the late fourteenth and late eighteenth centuries. This increase was approximately equivalent to the growth in population during that period. The rate of growth was even lower in the nineteenth century (with declining per capita output) and slightly less than 1 percent in the first half of the twentieth century (again, approximately equal to the rate of population growth).[3] Working within the confines of a traditional technology throughout this period, the Chinese were able to hold their own for over 500 years, but at an *average* annual rate of increase far below 2 percent.

Perkins estimates that approximately half of the increase in productivity between the beginning of the fifteenth century and the middle of the nineteenth century resulted from increases in the

[3]Dwight H. Perkins, *Agricultural Development in China, 1368–1968,* Aldine, Chicago, 1969. See particularly the discussion in Chapter II. Much of the quantitative information in the following paragraphs comes from this source and from Dwight H. Perkins, "Constraints Influencing China's Agricultural Performance," in *China: A Reassessment of the Economy,* pp. 350–365.

cultivated area. Yet, "by the nineteenth century, China had begun to run out of readily cultivatable land" and although "the amount of cultivated land increased about 40 percent in the hundred years prior to 1957, . . . about 80 percent of this increase was onto low quality land in Manchuria, Inner Mongolia, and elsewhere in the northwest."[4] Thus, this major source of increased agricultural productivity had been depleted in the six centuries before 1949; efforts to increase output since 1949 have concentrated on an attempt to increase yields, largely within the framework of a traditional technology.

The annual output estimates for agricultural production do not reveal either an upward or a downward trend in the approximate annual rate of increase of 2 percent that has prevailed since 1949. As has already happened in the case of increases in cultivated areas, the ability to sustain steady increases in output by raising yields *within* the traditional pattern of agricultural production may also soon encounter severely diminishing returns. Perkins estimates that the increased double cropping of wheat and barley and the introduction of new crops (corn and potatoes) that could thrive on poorer land accounted for one-fourth to one-third of the total increase in output over the last six centuries. Double cropping, however, has already been widely introduced throughout China, and by the 1950s there were few, if any, *new* crops that could be introduced to increase yields.

Nor does mechanization appear to offer a means for increasing agricultural productivity. Approximately 80 percent of China's large population lives in rural areas, and the rural labor force is estimated to have grown by 20 percent over the last 15 years alone. Mechanization that threatened the livelihoods of the peasants would be unlikely to be acceptable to the Chinese leadership. Perhaps its major contribution would be to assist in those tasks that cause the greatest demand for labor in the cyclical process of cultivation—transplanting, harvesting, and threshing — and often lead to shortages of labor.[5] The usefulness of mechanization would thus be its capacity to reduce the heavy burden of

[4]Perkins, *Agricultural Development*, p. 27.

[5]The importance of reducing the labor required by these peak-time tasks is that doing so removes a serious constraint on the number of crops that can be handled by a given amount of labor.

labor borne by the Chinese peasant and free that person for work on other agricultural tasks or for full-time employment in other parts of the economy, rather than its ability to secure significant increases in yields.

In recent years, the largest source of increased yields undoubtedly has been chemical fertilizer. China's traditional agricultural system was able to achieve relatively high yields by relying on widespread application of organic fertilizer (manure, nightsoil, beancakes, and compost), which probably provides as much as 75 kilograms of nutrient per hectare. Future increases in yield, however, will depend on very significant increases in the application of chemical fertilizer. Production and imports have increased the domestic supply of chemical fertilizer rapidly over the past decade;[6] the Chinese are now able to apply as much as 50 kilograms of nutrient per hectare from this source. Yet this is only one-sixth the amount the Japanese used for their crops more than a decade ago. In the United States, a single crop of rice receives 120 kilograms. Since more than one-half of China's cultivated area has multiple cropping, its needs would be greater yet. China would need to increase domestic supplies of chemical fertilizer by between three- and fourfold in order to apply an amount comparable to that used in countries with high yields in agriculture.

In the early 1970s China purchased 13 fertilizer plants that produce ammonia and urea. When these plants begin operation over the next few years, China will produce more than double the amount of nitrogen manufactured in 1974.[7] These plants cost a

[6]China was the world's largest importer of nitrogen fertilizer in 1972, but despite its need for much greater domestic supplies, these imports declined in 1973 and 1974 because of skyrocketing prices in the international fertilizer market and China's growing balance of payments problems. Given the Chinese leaders' substantial dislike of dependence on foreign sources of supply and the very large gap between domestic supplies of and demand for chemical fertilizer, when China did become the world's largest importer of this commodity in 1972, the leadership decided late that year to purchase 13 of the world's largest ammonia-urea fertilizer complexes.

[7]Information in this paragraph is taken from Alva Lewis Erisman, "China: Agriculture in the 1970's," in *China: A Reassessment of the Economy*, pp. 324–329; and CIA, *People's Republic of China: Chemical Fertilizer Supplies, 1949–1974*, A(ER)75-70, August 1975.

total of more than 650 million U.S. dollars, but the cost of increasing chemical fertilizer output is only one of the major problems the Chinese will encounter in their attempt to obtain increased yields from this source. Transportation problems loom large in plans to distribute the fertilizer to the farmers, because of both the limited capacity of transportation facilities (especially trucks and closed-container rail cars) and significant losses in nitrogen content during transport. Therefore, the new plants are being located in major agricultural areas in the interior of the country. Moreover, the Chinese have pursued a campaign of developing small-scale chemical fertilizer plants that not only reduce the burden in the transportation system but also utilize local deposits of raw materials. These small-scale plants now account for over one-half of China's current production of nitrogen. The output of these small plants, however, is of poorer quality than that of the large-scale, modern industrial sector: it consists mostly of ammonium bicarbonate, which is both relatively low in nitrogen content (compared with 46 percent for urea) and unstable. Finally, a major deficiency in China's supply of chemical fertilizer is the fertilizer's mix of nutrients. While the optimum mix is 100 parts of nitrogen to 50 of phosphorous and 33 of potassium, China's mix is commonly closer to 100 to 46 to 6. (Although China does have large potash deposits in the Western provinces, they are uneconomical to exploit because of prohibitive transport costs.)

By allocating the necessary investments, the Chinese can continue to acquire needed raw materials, develop production facilities, and construct a transportation network over the next 15 years that will enable them to increase the use of chemical fertilizer at the average annual rate of 20 percent that has obtained for the past two decades. This rate of increase would require them to increase the domestic supply of chemical fertilizer more than fourfold in the next 15 years. The major problem the Chinese face, however, is in using this increased supply of fertilizers without encountering seriously declining yield responses (i.e., increases in output per unit of nutrient added).[8] Based on a study

[8]Under suitable, but not necessarily ideal, conditions, a conservative estimate for yield responses (increase in output per unit increase in *nutrient*

of fertilizer responses in 40 countries, Williams and Couston estimate a (rice) yield response of 19.5 kilograms of grain (per kilogram of fertilizer) for the first 50 kilograms of nutrient (nitrogen), 8.2 for the next 50 kilograms of nutrient, and 6.4 for the next 50 kilograms of nutrient.[9] Furthermore, if fertilizer is to be effective, the cultivator must know how to use it, combine its application with the use of seeds that are highly responsive to fertilizer, and provide the sufficient amount of water at the right time.

The Chinese peasants have accumulated a vast storehouse of information over the past six centuries or more within the confines of their traditional agricultural techniques. Agricultural handbooks about the types of new seeds and chemical fertilizer and how to use them for various crops grown on different soils are readily available throughout China. Demonstration plots, discussion meetings, and technical experts sent down to the countryside reinforce the dissemination of this new information. Most of these improved seeds, however, are merely the result of the application of seeds proven superior in one area of China to other agricultural areas. An American delegation of plant scientists that visited China in 1974 believes that the Chinese neither rationally organize nor devote enough resources to the experimentation and basic research that would have the potential to produce increases in yields in the manner of a Green Revolution.

Another major obstacle that the Chinese must confront if they are to solve their agricultural problem is the storage and control of water—a necessary complement for achieving the potential yield

---

application) would be approximately 8 to 1. It has been argued that much of the increase in China's grain output between 1957 and 1974 can be attributed to the increased supply of chemical fertilizer that was specifically allocated to those areas where the suitable conditions (water and seeds) were present. See Benedict Stavis, *Making Green Revolution: The Politics of Agricultural Development in China*, Cornell University Press, Ithaca, N.Y., 1974; Jung-chau Liu, *China's Fertilizer Economy*, Aldine, Chicago, 1970; and Dwight Perkins, "Constraints," in *China: A Reassessment of the Economy*.

[9]Liu, *China's Fertilizer Economy*, p. 113.

response catalyzed by increased supplies of chemical fertilizer. Water control projects have long been an important governmental duty, as they were even prior to the unification of China in the third century B.C. In fact, Karl Witfogel argues that the political system that evolved in China over the past 22 centuries, which he terms "Oriental despotism," was partly a reaction to the need to construct and manage these projects that were essential to China's traditional agriculture. Chinese gazetteers list over 50,000 such projects, and there can be little doubt that they were an important element in the ability of Chinese traditional agriculture to support a large population with its limited cultivatable land area. It was the existence of these water control and irrigation networks, mostly in the southern area, where rainfall levels are sufficiently high and dependable, that allowed for extensive double cropping in China's traditional agriculture. In any event, by the beginning of this century more than one-fourth of China's cultivated acreage was irrigated. By the 1930s, most cultivatable land that had no serious problems of water supply had been irrigated.

Over the past 25 years, the Chinese have increased the irrigated acreage significantly by utilizing flood control projects, wells, and electric pumps. They completed the irrigation network in South China, expanded the irrigation and double-cropping (rice) network northward into Central China (north of the Yangtze River), and increased the irrigated acreage in the Southwest and Northeast (Manchuria). A delegation of American water management specialists who visited China in 1974 concluded that the ability of the Chinese to further develop irrigation in rice-growing areas was severely limited.

The rice-growing areas of the South, however, do not pose the most serious agricultural problems to the Chinese leadership. These areas have adequate and dependable supplies of water, are irrigated, and have been provided with the new and rapidly growing supplies of chemical fertilizers. As a result, rice yields are very high and fairly stable in this region: in the late 1950s, rice yields in Szechwan, China's rice bowl, were still approximately 25 percent below those in Japan, but were higher than those in Taiwan and Korea and more than double those in India, Thailand,

and Indonesia.[10] In other words, where the Chinese have developed the necessary complement of inputs, the results have been impressive and undoubtedly have contributed significantly to China's ability to maintain its average annual 2 percent rate of increase in agricultural output. Although continued investments in these inputs are likely to encounter the problem of diminishing returns in the short term, the outcome will still be more growth.

The agricultural picture in the North China Plain, China's traditional agricultural center and the home for over one-fifth of its population, is quite different. Here the farming is dry-land wheat growing; water supplies are inadequate and undependable, and yields are, on the average, relatively low and unstable.[11] When the rains are plentiful, floods occur. The major river on the North China Plain is estimated to carry 37 times the quantity of silt per cubic meter in its lower reaches than does the Nile, which makes water control and irrigation projects difficult, costly, and often inefficient. When the rains are insufficient, droughts occur and the Yellow River itself can even dry up. In fact, the rains are so undependable in both quantity and timing that both floods and droughts can occur in the same agricultural year.

To provide for sufficient and dependable supplies of water, the Chinese have undertaken the Yellow River Project, one of the most massive and comprehensive water control and irrigation projects in history. To prevent floods, a series of storage dams will be built on the upper reaches of the river to regulate its flow. To alleviate the serious silting problem, simultaneous, if not prior, erosion control in wastelands through which the river runs will be implemented. Finally, facilities will be created for the

[10] In an unpublished paper, Dwight Perkins argues that rice yields in China are now as high as those in Japan. These comparisons, however, are somewhat open to question. Yields in Japan, India, and Taiwan are probably reported on the basis of a single crop, while those for China probably are for the total year's output. Because of the new cropping patterns (intercropping, more transplanting, etc.) being introduced in Chinese agriculture, the yield per crop, according to the Chinese themselves, is declining; but because of the increase in the number of crops, the annual yield is increasing.

[11] At the end of the 1950s, wheat yields in China were approximately one-half the level of wheat yields in the United States. The contrast between the Chinese success in developing wheat and rice production is amply reflected in the Chinese net exports of rice and net imports of wheat over the past two decades.

continuous removal of silt from the river throughout its entire length.[12] Because of the relatively low and undependable flow of water in the Yellow River, even at the end of the 10 to 20 years that planners expect will be needed to complete the Yellow River Project, the addition to irrigated land would be 3.33 million hectares, or the equivalent of approximately 7.5 percent of China's irrigated acreage in 1974. This clearly indicates the tremendous costs involved in irrigating even that portion of the North China Plain along the Yellow River.

Another source of water for irrigating the North China Plain, and the one that has been considerably utilized by the Chinese over the past 25 years, is tube wells with power pumps that tap the ground water.[13] The use of these wells, however, must be coordinated with the supply of surface water from other irrigation projects, such as the Yellow River Project. A concentration of these wells or their extensive use would lower the water table and reduce the water available downriver. Thus, it is not just the construction but also the management and use of these irrigation projects in the North China Plain that require a large-scale and well-coordinated effort to obtain the high and stable yields these projects are intended to provide.[14]

[12]The host of a delegation visiting the Yellow River Exhibit Hall at Chengchow was considerably annoyed when members pressed him for statistics on the reduction of silt in the river resulting from the erosion control projects he had described in detail. His answer indicated that he was in the position of a man trying to put out a forest fire with a bucket of water who was asked to stop and estimate what effect it was having; it revealed his explicit faith that if enough people could be organized with buckets and kept working long enough, the fire would eventually be put out.

[13]According to the data collected by Dwight Perkins, there was no significant increase in irrigated acreage between the mid-1950s and the mid-1960s, and the share of total arable land that was irrigated in the mid-1950s was 31 percent, compared with 27 percent in the 1930s. Between the mid-1960s and mid-1970s, however, the amount of irrigated acreage was increased by almost one-third and the share of irrigated land in total arable land increased to over 40 percent. During this same period, the number of tube wells with power pumps increased thirteenfold. See Table 6 in Perkins, "Constraints" in *China: A Reassessment of the Economy*, p. 360.

[14]As suggested by Dwight Perkins, more dependable but much more expensive sources of water would be the Yangtze River (13 times the volume of flow of the Yellow River) and the Huai River (3 times the volume of flow of the

There is no doubt, as Dwight Perkins has argued, that the tremendous "outpouring of effort and resources" in agriculture during the 1960s and 1970s led not to a comparable leap in farm output, but only to a rate of increased agricultural productivity that was slightly above the rate of population growth. "The main reason why agricultural growth has not been faster appears to be simply that China is attempting to achieve large farm output increases under basically unfavorable conditions....[and] no major breakthrough appears in sight."[15] Because of both these unfavorable conditions and the diminishing returns from further additions of inputs, even greater efforts will be necessary to sustain the growth rates achieved in the past.

Evaluating the evidence and arguments similar to those used in Perkins' analyses, Alva Lewis Erisman reaches an almost identical conclusion. "Before 1972, PRC programs for agricultural development hinged primarily on one-time improvements in traditional agricultural practices or were subject to sharply diminishing returns. These improvements did not build a foundation for sustained growth."[16] Erisman argues that if inputs are provided in "an optimumly proportioned package," there is a possibility for sustained growth, but at a rate of approximately 2 percent.

It is possible that a recent major policy decision regarding agricultural development which was made and publicized after Perkins and Erisman made their projections could undermine the conclusion that agricultural growth over the next 15 years will, at best, exceed the rate of population growth by a slight margin. The Chinese, obviously cognizant both of arguments similar to those above and of the serious implications of these arguments for the

---

Yellow River) in Central China. Thus, the Chinese face the expensive choice of pumping water from Central China to the North China Plain. Given the desperate need to obtain high and stable yields, however, they are reported to have begun work on a project designed to divert water from the Huai River to the north.

[15] Perkins, "Constraints," in *China: A Reassessment of the Economy*, p. 365.

[16] Erisman, "China: Agriculture in the 1970's" in *China: A Reassessment of the Economy*, p. 348.

Chinese economic development program, believe they have now adopted an approach that will solve the agricultural problem.[17]

This large-scale effort involves the identification of "model communes" that are achieving rapid increases in yields. Selection of models for emulation has been a popular instrument of policy implementation in China over the past 25 years. The most famous of these model communes (actually a brigade) is Tachai. In 1964, Mao suggested that "in agriculture, learn from Tachai"; this slogan is prominently displayed in large characters almost everywhere in rural China (on mountains, dams, buildings, etc.) as well as frequently referred to in newspapers, journals, and radio broadcasts. It was only after a meeting of agricultural specialists and political leaders in 1970, however, that the spread of the Tachai model to other selected areas of North China gained any significance. I spent three days at the Tachai Production Brigade in the summer of 1975. From the lovely pattern of terraced fields of corn—restructured from the reddish, barren hills—to the new public housing and equalitarian incentive system, the Tachai Brigade is indeed a unique and impressive experiment in rural China. The Tachai Brigade, however, is not just a matter of curiosity, a unique example of a relatively small group of peasants struggling to overcome the harsh constraints of

[17]While visiting China as a member of the Small-Scale Industries Delegation in the summer of 1975 and discussing the problem of the "iron law" of diminishing returns and the difficulty of increasing output continuously through increased applications of inputs, I received a lengthy lecture in terminology more common to propaganda releases than to economic analysis. Realizing my inability to understand the true meaning of what was being said, I was given an answer that not only revealed a good grasp of neoclassical economics (the speaker had taught economics at Yenan during World War II) but Chinese faith in the future as well. "We know all about economics, but the problem with Western economists is their concentration on static equilibrium theory where movements along a *given* production function (the condition of diminishing returns) is the source of increased output. In the dynamic real world, however, things are not given and history tells us the major sources of increases in output over time come from continuous outward shifts in the production function. Why shouldn't that be true for China." Good point and a major reason why I hesitate to accept uncritically the conclusions of the two authors presented above in the text.

their environment. Rather, it represents a broad-ranging and interdependent set of policies that is to be studied as the "model" for possible transfer and application throughout China.[18]

A brief summary of the major features of the Tachai model which are to be transferred elsewhere indicates the bold and radical nature of the agricultural transformation being sought. Regarding leadership, Tachai emphasizes the politically reliable old-style guerrilla fighter (as against the specialist) whose expertise is in mobilizing and leading the masses in an all-out war to modernize agriculture and achieve higher yields. Regarding organization and incentive, Tachai emphasizes the larger socialist units of production (the brigade as against the smaller team), whose members work in a collectivist spirit of cooperation and initiative rather than for task-related individual material rewards.

The farmland is remolded into bigger and level fields to allow for the introduction of mechanization and irrigation. Major water control and irrigation projects are undertaken in order to collect water from all available sources (rainfall, spring runoff, rivers, or underground pools and flow), to provide facilities for the storage of water, and to distribute it to the fields.[19] Land reclamation is also important, with spring water runoff channels and rivers being moved underground through man-made tunnels of considerable length. Cropping patterns are also changed. For example, where water is made available, higher-yield rice replaces wheat

[18]In its role as a model, the Tachai Brigade receives over 2,000 Chinese visitors daily and has had as many as 30,000 in a single day.

[19]These projects were among the most impressive things I observed during my trip to China. Even though one would have to assume that the real wage and interest rates were close to zero (the opportunity costs of labor and capital were very small) to justify their construction in a traditional cost-benefit analysis, one could not help but admire the Red Flag Canal (which brought water to Lin County from a river a considerable distance away in another province), children in the mountains chipping rocks for construction of a large water storage tank, and underground dams to trap the underground flow of water. The latter project was sprung on us after a long, hot, dusty, bumpy ride into the Taihang Mountains to a barren, rocky gully. Standing in the gully, we were told we were standing over a large underground dam, and we were taken down a well in which we observed the trapped water being pumped through pipes that carried it to the agricultural fields several miles away.

and corn, and intercropping is introduced to make more efficient use of the available sunlight and land to lengthen the annual period in which crop growth may take place. Also it is now quite common to see short crops (soybeans) intercropped with tall crops (corn) and corn intercropped with wheat.[20]

Small-scale industries relying on local financing, raw materials, and labor are constructed to supply the cement, chemical fertilizer, electricity, and agricultural machinery required in this program of agricultural transformation. Mechanization is sought to increase the labor supply so as to meet the large increase in demand for labor resulting from the farmland construction, the change in cropping pattern (i.e., rice growing, intercropping, and greater double cropping), and the small-scale, rural industrialization program. Electrification is carried out to mechanize the threshing floors and food processing (grain milling), which now place a very heavy demand on labor. Finally, technical information concerning all aspects of this agricultural transformation is disseminated to the peasants, who at the same time are urged to innovate and experiment. Scientists and technicians are expected to work with the masses to seek short-run solutions to practical problems rather than to engage in basic research.

The results of these efforts on a few model communes are very impressive. For example, average grain yields at Tachai increased from approximately 0.75 tons per acre in 1953, to 2.5 tons in 1963, to almost 3.5 tons in 1973.[21] Some rice has been grown at Tachai since 1973 with yields of over 5 tons per acre. Obviously impressed with the results of the Tachai experiment, the State Council convened a nationwide conference of 3,700 representatives at Tachai on September 15, 1975. The national and local representatives attending this conference were told they

[20]Soybeans maintain the structure of the soil and can be planted or harvested late in the season without reducing yields very much. The intercropping of corn and wheat can increase total annual yields by as much as 40 percent.

[21]Yields at Tachai reached a peak in 1971 and remained relatively stable at a level slightly below that peak in 1972 and 1973 because of drought conditions that continued through 1974 and 1975.

were to visit Tachai to observe what had been accomplished there, to learn the lessons of that experience, and to decide how to promote and popularize, *as quickly as possible*, the building of Tachai-type agricultural units throughout the country. Hua Kuo-feng's report summarizing the conference was entitled "Mobilize the Whole Party, Make Greater Efforts to Develop Agriculture and Strive to Build Tachai-Type Counties Throughout the Country"; this same theme was repeated in the *Renmen Ribao* editorial on October 21, 1975.[22] Party organizations at all levels were instructed to make every effort to introduce the Tachai model throughout the country during the spring and winter of 1976. These instructions were obviously directed to solving China's agricultural problem on the North China Plain; the target date for that region was set at 1980.

The essential question, of course, is the extent to which the adoption of this sweeping campaign will result in productivity that surpasses the estimated annual rate of increase of 2 percent over the next 15 years. Total grain output at Tachai increased by 6 percent a year between 1963 and 1973. It is important to note, however, that most of this increase resulted from a significant shift to the production of rice (a higher-yield crop) rather than from increases in yields *per* crop, which generally depend on the availability of water. Furthermore, the success of Tachai is greatly dependent on several other factors that are not likely to be readily available in sufficient quantities throughout the North China Plain: a strong, dynamic, guerrilla-type leadership (veterans from pre-1949 guerrilla fighting in the civil war); considerable resources and heavy spring water runoff in the surrounding mountains; and the critical investment of both physical and financial capital as well as technical and labor assistance that Peking provided to ensure the success of the Tachai model.[23]

[22]The unit chosen for the transfer of the Tachai model is the *county*, not the commune. This is important because the county represents "state" ownership and control, whereas the commune is part of the cooperative sector.

[23]This is the impression obtained in observing the Tachai model first hand. It is illustrated by the fact that grain sold to the state was at the same level in 1973 as it had been in 1963, a large water reservoir and aqueduct system was built with the "assistance" of the PLA, many of the projects and small-scale industries

Thus, the possibility of switching from wheat to rice on the North China Plain will depend on that area's large-scale and coordinated water control projects. For this reason, the new "learn from Tachai" campaign in China is unlikely to modernize Chinese agriculture over the next 15 years—except in those areas "blessed" with the necessary leadership, resources, sources of water, and outside help.[24] I therefore think that the estimate of 2 percent annual rate of growth for Chinese agriculture remains accurate.[25] In other words, the Chinese are unlikely to achieve a

---

involved considerable inputs of both technical expertise and scarce resources supplied from outside, and the population of trucks and agricultural machinery was relatively higher in Tachai than on the North China plain. The same was true for the use of chemical fertilizer. These observations should not downgrade the importance of the strenuous efforts of the local inhabitants as well as their ingenuity and initiative; however, they do indicate that a critical "margin" of assistance helped make the Tachai experiment successful.

[24]Inasmuch as the campaign has just begun, this rather strongly stated conclusion should be taken as the author's intuitive judgment only. This year (1976–1977) I am devoting full time at the University of Michigan to explore this judgment more fully, thanks to a grant from the Chinese Economics Project (Mellon Foundation).

[25]There is an explanation of what may appear to be an inconsistency in my argument: I have argued that the Chinese will find it increasingly difficult to diversify the means used in the past to obtain agricultural growth (i.e., irrigation, double cropping, etc.) and that the marginal productivity of current inputs (i.e., fertilizer, etc.) will decline as their level of use increases. Yet my conclusion is that agricultural growth in the future is likely to remain what it has been over the past decade. These arguments and the conclusion are compatible for the following reasons. Although given increases in agricultural output will become more difficult (i.e., more costly), the Chinese have already decided to devote these resources for that purpose in a much greater scale in the future than in the past. Although the marginal productivity of current inputs on each piece of land declines with increases in the level of inputs used, the growth of agricultural output throughout China in the past was due, in large part, to the increase of these inputs in certain parts of China. Thus, diminishing returns will become an important problem in those areas, but Chinese agriculture contains many areas where the use of these inputs has a relatively high marginal productivity. Quite simply, although we expect the returns obtained, on the average, from a given amount of investment and effort in Chinese agriculture in the future to be smaller than in the past, the increase in the total scale of efforts and the attempt to create a more balanced and complementary mix of inputs over a larger area is expected to enable the Chinese to maintain a rate of growth in total agriculture approximately equal to that of the past.

breakthrough in their attempts to solve their economic problem. Agricultural development will continue to be a severe constraint on overall economic growth and on significant increases in the standard of living of the Chinese people.

INDUSTRY

Increases in industrial production are obtained by increasing either the amount of physical capital, raw materials, and labor used for production or the productivity of these inputs. Since China is adequately endowed with raw materials and labor supply, the dominant constraint on its industrial development is the need to maintain its recent rate of investment in physical capital. The significant industrial growth since 1949 was made possible by a very high rate of investment.[26] Over the next 15 years, however, the Chinese will have greater difficulty in maintaining both that high rate of investment and, more important, the rate of return on that investment.

Although a host of arguments can lead to this conclusion, only the signal reasons will be presented here. The damping of the rate of investment will result from the pressures tending to increase the rate of consumption. Because of rationing and the relatively stable real wages that have existed for the past few decades, considerable pent-up demand undoubtedly exists for higher standards of living. If the government is to continue to use material incentives, it will have to effect a steady increase in those standards in order to obtain increases in productivity. Since agricultural production is growing only slightly faster than population, rapid increases in manufactured consumer goods, especially durables such as bicycles, sewing machines, watches,

[26]Gross domestic capital formation accounted for approximately one-fourth of gross domestic product during the 1950s; more than one-half of this capital accumulation occurred in the industrial sector. Reliable data are not available for the 1960s or 1970s, but the Chinese undoubtedly maintained an investment rate above 20 percent and although agriculture has enjoyed a much higher priority since the 1950s, approximately 40 percent of total investment must still go to industry.

radios, etc., may alleviate this problem somewhat but will not solve it.

The source of the demand for a higher standard of living is found in both the industrial and the agricultural sectors. Nonetheless, the fact that industrial workers already enjoy a *relatively* high standard of living has forced Peking to control strictly the rate of migration from the rural areas to the urban industrial centers. Although the recent drive to create rural, small-scale industries has reduced the rural-urban differences in income levels, it has not significantly altered the differences in income between industrial and agricultural workers.[27] The *relatively* low standard of living of the average Chinese peasant, its slow rate of growth, the long-standing promise of equitable income distribution, and the necessity to sustain both the labor effort and political loyalty of the peasants will create a pressure that the Chinese leadership will be unable to deny to devote a greater share of the total GNP to consumption.

Whatever the *rate* of investment in the future, the growing importance of several alternative claims on investment will tend to reduce the *share* that has been allocated to industry—especially the producer goods sector—over the past 25 years. The higher priority of agriculture will result not only in a smaller share of investment for industry, but also in a much greater percentage of that share going to industries that produce inputs for agriculture—chemical fertilizer, agricultural machinery, irrigation pumps, etc. A significant percentage of these goods will be produced in rural, small-scale industries developed through investment at the local (especially the county) level. However, this greater share of investment at the local level will reduce the investment that might be made in the modern industrial sector by the central government.

Other budget items will also reduce the investment funds

[27]This statement refers to national averages and does not include those individual cases of communes that have become quite prosperous and whose members enjoy a standard of living quite similar to that of industrial workers. Most of these prosperous communes are to be found in the rural areas surrounding large metropolitan centers; thus they have large markets close by in which to sell their subsidiary products.

available for the industrial sector. Among these are increasing expenditures on public consumption and social overhead capital, such as hospital and medical facilities, educational facilities, and public housing projects. Although there has been rapid growth over the past 25 years, much still remains to be done.[28] Transportation facilities—including the rail, river, and highway network—will also have to be maintained, improved, and increased, not simply to keep pace with industrial development but to alleviate the existing problems as well. The lack of adequate transportation facilities has caused serious problems for the coordination of distribution and supply which can be expected to increase when the output of the rural, small-scale industries exceeds the needs of the local area. With the share of investment thus reduced, the rate of growth of industrial production is also likely to decline in comparison with the rates of the past 25 years.

Finally, whatever the share of investment allocated to industry, the annual output per unit of investment will also decline because of the shift in favor of the more capital-intensive industries and the modernization of existing industries. Having developed its basic industries to the point where it is relatively self-sufficient in energy, basic machine tools, and metals, China requires in the future the development of industries with significantly higher capital-output ratios. According to a study of China's energy consumption in 1966–1974, each 1 percent increase in GNP required a 1.42 percent increase in energy supplies (meaning a GNP elasticity of 1.42).[29] The provision of this supply will depend much more than it has previously on the extraction and processing of petroleum and the harnessing of hydroelectric power potential. Even the continued expansion of the coal industry will depend on the use of more modern mining and refining equipment for the more intensive exploitation of China's huge coal resources, rather than on the earlier labor-intensive methods.

[28]Much of this public consumption is provided for by local units in China—especially the commune and the factory. Nonetheless, investments at this level still reduce the potential for investment in the modern industrial sector.

[29]CIA, *China: Energy Balance Projections*, A(ER)75-75, November 1975, p. 14.

In the machine-building and metal industries, the prospects are similar. Continued economic development with a higher number of continuous production runs, more production of standardized parts, higher-quality and precision products, and more "automation" will increase the already existing demand for a greater amount and variety of task-specific, precision, complicated machinery, such as headless, precision grinders rather than basic surface grinders. These machines will be required not only to equip factories that will be constructed in the future but also to modernize most existing factories. Some of these machines are already produced in China in limited numbers, but the scale of production must be increased significantly.

A unique feature of Chinese industry is the creation of construction, maintenance and repair, and equipment-production facilities within each factory. A significant portion of the capital accumulation and modernization in the industrial sector is provided by these machine shops that produce their own equipment, which tends to be the more basic or standard pieces. The task of the modern machine-building sector will be to create a domestic supply capability for the more sophisticated machinery and equipment that China's economic development will require.

Among these needs for machinery and equipment are the demands of China's defense establishment, agricultural sector, transportation sector, and the rapidly growing chemical industry (fertilizer and synthetic fibers). Even if China hopes to maintain only a conventional, *but modern*, military force, it would require the production of the most modern and up-to-date aircraft, ships, and weaponry. Any attempt to develop and maintain even a limited missile system with nuclear capabilities would involve relatively high capital and skilled labor costs, not to mention research and development expenditures. The larger and more efficient of the agricultural machinery plants in the rural industrial sector are equipped with modern machinery and are introducing assembly-line serial production. Engines for larger pieces of agricultural machinery are produced in the modern, large-scale industrial sector, where the capital-labor ratio is higher than the average ratio for all Chinese industry. The transportation sector has a great need for trucks and equipment used in building and repairing roads. The production of these goods—an area in which the Chinese have been beset by problems of effective operation—must also be greatly expanded. China's development of the transportation system also will lead to the production on a larger scale of diesel engines, tank cars (for petroleum), and sealed-container carriers (for aqueous ammonia).

In the metal industry, serious bottlenecks remain in the production of finished rolled steel—a very important product in an industrialized country—and of high-quality alloys. Furthermore, the attempt to increase the variety and quality of metal products will require the development of purification and benefication facilities for improving the quality of the raw materials (iron ore and coal).

The above discussion assumes that the Chinese will attempt to increase not only the absolute level of these capital-intensive industrial products but also the proportion of these products in the total industrial output. A desire to develop these industries was clearly reflected in China's import trade during the early 1970s. In 1970–1974, China's imports of machinery and equipment grew at an annual average of 44 percent, reaching a level of 1.7 billion U.S. dollars in 1974 and equaling approximately one-fourth of China's total imports.[30] These imports totaled almost 4 billion U.S. dollars over this five-year period. More than two-thirds of these imports came from the non-Communist industrialized countries and the Soviet Union; in 1970–1973, over 50 percent of China's imports of machinery and equipment from these countries consisted of transportation equipment (road vehicles, aircraft, and railway vehicles). Between 1970 and 1974, the Chinese imported approximately 35 million tons of chemical fertilizers, or approximately 25 percent of their total supply. These needs made China the world's largest importer of chemical fertilizer during the 1970s. During the same period, China's imports of minerals and metals were more than 5.5 billion U.S. dollars, or more than one-fourth of its total imports.

[30]Nai-ruenn Chen, "China's Foreign Trade, 1950–1974," in *China: A Reassessment of the Economy*, op. cit, pp. 617–652; and CIA, *Foreign Trade in Machinery and Equipment since 1952*, A(ER)75-60, January 1975. Data in the remainder of this paragraph are also from these sources.

The rapid growth in the 1970s of these imports of machinery and equipment, chemical fertilizers, and metals, combined with the constraints on China's export capacity, soon resulted in a serious balance-of-payments problem. Thus, the emphasis on a development policy of self-dependency was reinforced by the growing demand for these industrial commodities; as a result, the Chinese began to purchase complete plants abroad to provide for domestic production of these commodities. During 1973 and 1974, they signed agreements with the industrialized countries calling for the delivery and construction during the remainder of the 1970s of complete plants worth more than 2 billion U.S. dollars. Most of these plants were for the chemical (synthetic cloth and fibers and chemical fertilizer), metals (hot and cold rolling mills and steel-plating plants), and petroleum industries. All these industries, of course, are relatively capital-intensive.

It is not a simple matter to estimate the net effect of these tendencies in the rate, allocation, and productivity of investment on the rate of growth of industrial output in China over the next 15 years. The Chinese industrial labor force undoubtedly will benefit from "learning by doing," which will result in significant increases in productivity. Nonetheless, I believe the impact of these tendencies may seriously affect China's rate of growth, leading to declines similar to those experienced by the Soviet Union and countries of Eastern Europe as they shifted from extensive to intensive industrial development almost 20 years ago.[31]

Evidence that such a decline may occur can also be found in China's development over the past 25 years; simple regression of

[31] Reviewing economic growth in the Soviet Union and Eastern Europe, Thad D. Alton notes that capital productivity rates of growth became negative in these countries during 1961–1967. For 1961–1965, decreases in capital productivity were − 15 percent for the Soviet Union, − 24 percent for Bulgaria, − 6 percent for Hungary, − 17 percent for Czechoslovakia, and − 10 percent for East Germany. In East Germany, for each 1,000-mark increase in the capital stock, national income increased 656 marks in 1951–1955, 333 marks in 1956–1960, and 162 marks in 1961–1964. The incremental capital–national income ratio in Hungary was 2.12 in 1958–1960 but 3.9 in 1961–1965. See Thad P. Alton, "Economic Structure and Growth in Eastern Europe," in *Economic Development in Countries of Eastern Europe*, Studies Prepared for the Joint Economic Committee, Congress of the United States, Washington, D.C., 1970, p. 64.

the 25 annual rates of growth in industrial production over that period indicates a declining trend of one-half a percentage point per year, which is largely the result of prevailing average growth rates greater than 20 percent during the 1950s (rehabilitation and extensive growth) and less than 10 percent during the 1970s (intensive growth). One analyst believes that the Chinese will be able to maintain their recent moderate rate of growth of 8 to 10 percent in industrial development at least for the remainder of the decade. The major problems he foresees for the Chinese in this respect are "the ever present possibility of breakdown due to political disruption, worker discontent or a desperate attempt to accelerate the rate of growth."[32] These problems are a serious threat to China's industrial growth and will be discussed in the next section of this essay. Even if they are avoided, however, I believe that the rate of industrial growth will be reduced to an annual *average* of 6 to 8 percent over the next 15 years.

Before we move on to a discussion of the possible impact of unforeseen political developments or an unexpected change in development strategy on the estimated annual rate of growth of 2 percent in agricultural production and 7 percent in industrial production, several other aspects of China's future economic development must also be forecast.

CONSUMPTION

The Chinese leadership is likely to secure a modest, but positive, increase in the standard of living through the following economic policies, most of which have been implemented in recent years. Because of the excess demand for foodstuffs, the Chinese have increased the share of cultivated area devoted to food production and have reduced the share devoted to industrial and commercial crops;[33] they have also increased imports and reduced exports of

[32]Robert Michael Field, "Civilian Industrial Production in the People's Republic of China: 1949–1974," in *China: A Reassessment of the Economy*, pp. 159–160.

[33]"Despite its importance, the acreage of cotton has remained more or less constant over the past decade because of the higher priority assigned to grain."

foodstuffs, especially soybeans.[34] This shift in the cropping pattern, along with the use of rationing to enforce a more equitable distribution, has enabled the Chinese leadership to assure their people a daily intake of more than 2,000 calories. Thus, the gap between effective demand (due to relatively low and stable incomes) and supply of foodstuffs is probably within reasonable limits today. Yet the relatively slow growth in the production of foodstuffs and the need to allow for some increase in the standard of living means that a large-scale net import of foodstuffs will undoubtedly continue over the next 15 years.[35]

The constraints of domestic production and import capacity, however, mean that the increased standard of living cannot come from increased food supplies alone. Rather, the Chinese leadership, as in the past decade, can be expected to emphasize the importance of a rising share of public consumption (health, education, housing, etc.) and manufactured consumer goods (light industry). A significant shift in the allocation of investment from the producer to the consumer goods industries has already occurred in the last 10 years. During the 1950s, output in the producer goods industries was increasing at a rate four times as fast as that in the consumer goods industries; by the 1970s,

---

Alva Lewis Erisman, "China: Agriculture in the 1970's," in *China: A Reassessment of the Economy*, p. 341. Other industrial and commercial crops include oilseeds, fibers, sugar cane and beets, tobacco, soybeans, etc. There is good evidence to indicate that soybean output has been directly diverted to domestic food consumption in recent years to supplement the slow-growing output of food grains. See footnote 34 below.

[34] Grain imports averaged 5 million tons in 1970–1975. "Peking's agricultural policies in the early 1970s stimulated a rapid expansion of soybean acreage and output. . . . Most of China's current soybean output is believed to be consumed as a foodstuff rather than being exported or used for industrial purposes. Herein lies the reason Peking is again including soybeans as a grain. For example, China's soybean exports, almost all of which were shipped to Japan, averaged about 550,000 tons annually in 1965–1969. Although soybean output in 1974 and 1975 was probably more than double the 1965–69 average, Japan was only able to obtain delivery of one-half of the amount contracted for." CIA, *China: Agricultural Performance in 1975*, A(ER)76-10149, March 1976, p. 9.

[35] I expect that the average level of these net foodstuffs imports will increase *slightly faster* than population growth, but their level in any particular year, of course, will depend on the size of the harvest in that and the previous year.

however, the difference between these rates of growth had been cut in half. I expect this trend to continue, resulting in a rate of growth in the producer goods industries that will be only 50 percent greater than that in the consumer goods industries in 1975–1990. The structure of industry as a whole, of course, will continue to shift in favor of the producer goods industries over the next 15 years.[36] At the same time, however, the rate of growth of the consumer goods industries is likely to remain significantly larger than the increase in the standard of living; as well, the share of consumption derived from manufactured consumer goods is likely to increase steadily over the next 15 years.

Although I expect the ratio of the rate of growth of producer goods industrial output to that of consumer goods industrial output to be reduced to 1.5 to 1, both rates of growth are likely to decline from their levels of the past five years, falling to approximately 9 and 6 percent, respectively, as against 13 and 7 percent. The arguments for the lower level of growth in the producer goods industrial sector have already been presented above.[37] The reasons for the decline in the rate of growth of the consumer goods industrial sector are neither that sector's reduced share of investment nor higher marginal capital-output ratios so much as the constraints resulting from the slow growth in agriculture. Approximately three-fourths of the raw material needed to manufacture consumer goods consists of agricultural products. This dependence on agricultural products that are not readily available, such as cotton, tobacco, and other agricultural industrial crops, has kept consumer goods industries from operating at full capacity during lengthy periods over the past 25 years.

[36]The continued priority of the producer goods industries, although considerably reduced between the 1950s and 1970s, is borne out in the rural, small-scale industry campaign. Most of the rural, small-scale industries manufacture producer goods for agriculture; very few—except for grain-processing facilities—produce consumer goods.

[37]Those arguments were the lower share of investment in GDP, the lower share of investment going to industry, the lower share of investment in industry going to the producer goods industries, and the higher marginal capital-output ratio in the producer goods industries due to the changing structure of that sector, as well as the modernization and intensive development of existing industries.

Furthermore, to sustain required increases in food supplies, food crops have been given top priority in the allocation of cultivatable land. Yet producers of industrial and commercial crops have been given preference in the distribution of food grains and chemical fertilizers. Nonetheless, the rate of growth of industrial and commercial crops, especially cotton, oilseeds, sugar, and tobacco, has had difficulty in keeping pace with the relatively low rate of increase for food grains over the past 25 years.[38] China's inability to increase the production of industrial and commercial crops sufficiently to keep pace with the demand for them in industry is reflected in Peking's continued reliance on rather stringent rationing of textiles and edible oils and its growing dependence on imports of these commodities to maintain the increasing levels of industrial production of consumer goods.[39]

FOREIGN TRADE

Foreign trade will act as a major constraint on China's future economic development primarily because of the limits on China's ability to pay for its imports. Domestic supply and demand, of course, determine both China's export capacity and its needs for imports. China's exports are dominated by agricultural raw and processed products; the combination of the relatively low rate of

[38]Only scattered data are available for recent years. Available estimates for output in 1974 indicate the following average annual rates of increase since 1965: food grains, 2 percent; cotton, 3 percent; and sugar, 2 percent. CIA, *People's Republic of China: Handbook of Economic Indicators*, A(ER)75-72, August 1975, p. 3. No reports for recent years are available for oilseeds and tobacco, but in 1952–1957 (a period for which official data are available) the annual average rates of increase for these crops were 0.2 and 2.9 percent, respectively, compared with the average annual rate of increase for all agricultural crop production of 4.5 percent and the planned rate of increase for tobacco of 12.1 percent.

[39]The annual average levels of net imports of sugar and cotton (in thousand metric tons) were 86 and 11, respectively, in 1955–1957, 348 and 112.5 in 1962–1965, and 585 and 220 in 1971–1973. These data represent average annual rates of growth over the past two decades of 12 and 20 percent, respectively. Data on net imports from Erisman, "China: Agriculture in the 1970's," in *China: A Reassessment of the Economy*, p. 344.

growth of agricultural production and the need to increase the domestic standard of living has caused China's export capacity to grow relatively slowly.[40] China's domestic needs—its attempt to increase the standard of living and its growing consumer goods industries—have necessitated imports of both foodstuffs and industrial crops. Furthermore, the relatively high rates of investment and growth in heavy industry require that China import producer goods for the producer goods industries. Finally, the desire to stimulate agricultural production has caused China to import chemical fertilizer and other producer goods.

However, unless a benefactor supplies China with a continuous flow of foreign aid or foreigners are willing to make investments and reinvest their profits in China, in the long run the value of China's imports must equal the value of its exports. These sources of funds not only are unlikely to be found but also are unlikely to be desired by the Chinese even if they could be found. China is currently engaged in some short-run borrowing from abroad, but the necessity of repaying these loans would mean that its imports could not exceed its exports over a 15-year period. Long-term loans, which are a possibility, will be considered in Chapter Five. Currently, however, the Chinese are unwilling to engage in long-term borrowing from abroad, at least on any significant scale, in part because of their economically beneficial, but politically undesirable, experience with Soviet loans in the 1950s. In the long run, China's oil reserves offer an excellent source of exports for obtaining sizable foreign exchange earnings, another possibility that is discussed in Chapter Five. The *rapid* development of these reserves for export, however, would require—in the short run—increased imports of the machinery and equipment for extraction, refinement,

---

[40]In *real terms*, China's exports in 1952–1974 grew at an average annual rate of 5 percent. Most of this growth, however, occurred in the 1950s, when China's foreign trade was regaining its prewar peak levels. Between 1959 and 1974 China's exports increased, in real terms, by only 19 percent, or an annual average rate of increase of 1 percent. The growth trend between the period of 1955–1957 and the period 1972–1974 was approximately 3 percent. Nai-ruenn Chen, "China's Foreign Trade: 1950–1974," in *China: A Reassessment of the Economy*, p. 645.

transportation, and port facilities. In other words, while the export of oil may certainly alleviate the constraints imposed by the foreign trade sector on China's economic development, it will not eliminate them over the next 15 years.

Thus, we assume that the growth in China's foreign trade over the next 15 years will be constrained by the growth in exports and that, *on the average*, China's imports cannot exceed its exports. Despite China's record of industrialization over the past 25 years, raw and processed agricultural products (including textiles) still accounted for almost two-thirds of China's exports in the early 1970s. Exports of petroleum, chemical products, machinery and transport equipment, and miscellaneous manufactured goods have increased significantly but still account for only one-fifth of China's total exports in the 1970s, which increased by 7.5 percent (in constant prices) from 1969 to 1974. In other words, the slow growth of agricultural production will remain a serious constraint on the growth of China's export capacity, although exports of industrial products and petroleum undoubtedly will become increasingly important.

If the future trend in the growth rate for exports were to follow the likely decline in the growth rate forecast for the economy as a whole (compared with the rates of 1969–1974), China's total exports would grow at a 5 percent rate. For the period 1952–1974, the elasticity of export growth with respect to growth in GDP (percent change in exports divided by percent change in GDP) was 1.04; if this equation is applied to my forecast for growth in China's GDP over the next 15 years, the rate of growth of exports is projected at 5.2 percent. The elasticity of export growth with respect to the rate of growth in agriculture in 1952–1974 was 2.4; if this figure is applied to the forecasted rate of growth in China's agricultural production over the next 15 years, the rate of growth of exports would be 4.8 percent. Thus, assuming that there will be no changes in the Chinese leadership's current policies regarding foreign loans and investments or the proper level of self-dependency and foreign trade dependency, the likely rate of growth of China's foreign trade (both exports and imports) over the next 15 years is 5 percent. Whether or not this assumption is the most reasonable one to make, as well as what the possible effects of alternative assumptions on these forecasts would be, is discussed later in this study.

SUMMARY

The above arguments concerning the evolution of China's economy over the next 15 years are summarized in Table 1. Although the preceding discussion has referred continually to serious constraints the Chinese will encounter wherever they turn, the summary forecast in Table 1 represents a remarkably

TABLE 1

Summary of Forecasts: China's Economy in 1990*
(Absolute levels in billion constant 1975 U.S. dollars)

	1975–1990 Average Annual Growth in Percentages	1990 Index (1975 = 100)	Absolute	Percentage
GNP†	5	213	419.6	100
Agriculture	2	134	97.4	23
Industry	7	312	233.6	55
Consumer goods	6	239	73.1	17
Producer goods‡	9	364	160.5	38
Services§	4	180	88.6	21
Population	1.7	128	1,024	
Per capita consumption	3	155	138.8	
Foreign trade				
Exports	5	213	13.8	
Imports	5	213	13.8	
Foreign trade dependency¶			3%	

successful record of economic development. At a sustained rate of growth of 5 percent, China's GNP in 1990 would be more than double its present level and would be slightly larger than Japan's GNP in 1974. Per capita GNP would grow at a rate of 3.3 percent a year, achieving a level over 400 U.S. dollars per capita in 1990. Consumption would still be less than 50 percent of total GNP by 1990, but actual consumption per capita would increase by over 50 percent in the next 15 years and almost as quickly as per capita GNP. The relatively high rate of investment and industrial growth would continue the radical shift in the structure of the economy over the next 15 years, with industry accounting for over 50 percent of GNP by 1990. This industrialization will enable the Chinese to achieve satisfactory growth paths while pursuing self-dependency and will allow the foreign trade dependency ratio to remain at its already low level.

---

*Estimates presented here are obtained by selecting an approximate rate of growth derived from the analysis in Chapter Four and applying it to the absolute values for the relevant economic activity in the base year, 1975. The 1975 base year values are those presented in Robert F. Dernberger, "The Economic Consequences of Defense Expenditure Choices in China," in *China: A Reassessment of the Economy*, (section titled, "The Base Year: The Chinese Economy in 1975"), pp. 472–475.

†In evaluating the relative size of the various sectors, it should be remembered that the values of output in the various sectors are gross values, which means that outputs that are used as inputs in other industries in the same sector are counted twice, thereby overvaluing industrial production, especially producer goods, compared with output in the agricultural and service sector.

‡Includes the production of the military industries.

§Includes transportation, construction, trade, public utilities, government services, banking, and consumer services. Although public consumption is assumed to grow faster than 5 percent (population growth, plus increase in per capita consumption) so that it becomes a larger share of consumption expenditures, the service sector as a whole is expected to grow at a slower rate although still increasing in per capita terms.

¶Imports divided by GDP. This ratio makes sense when one is measuring the foreign trade dependency for China inasmuch as imports are restricted to those items that are viewed as essential for achieving GNP and that must be obtained from abroad. In market economies, a foreign trade involvement ratio is frequently calculated which shows the share of both imports and exports in total GNP. For China in 1990 this foreign trade involvement ratio would be 6 percent.

Nonetheless, per capita consumption will remain at a relatively low level, and the disparities in growth rates between agricultural and industrial development will continue as the major long-run problem in China's economic development. The most immediate problem, of course, is the threat of political instability. In deriving this forecast I have made several crucial assumptions about China's political and economic system and policies. In general, these assumptions called for moderation and stability, and the resulting forecast similarly presents a picture of stable growth. This stable growth path, however, will be a precarious one whose realization will depend greatly on the validity of those assumptions.

VALIDITY OF ASSUMPTIONS[41]

The forecast summarized in Table 1 is but a reflection of several crucial underlying assumptions. Therefore, a brief review and justification of those assumptions is in order before an estimate of the influence of China's future economic development on China's role in the international system can be made. These assumptions fall into three major categories: the economic parameters that identify and quantify the cause and effect relationships in the

[41]This section has been added to the revised version of the study in reaction to criticisms of an earlier draft. The previous sections in this part of the study present my "forecast" of the future evolution of the Chinese economy given what we *now* know about the past and present developments in China's economy and considering the various factors that will affect the economy in the future. The essential question I ask is this: What is the most reasonable *present* expectation of the *future* evolution of China's economy? Events unexpected *at present* will, of course, affect and change the actual results. Thus, some critics argued that it would be desirable to specify at least some of what those unexpected events might be and also to speculate on what their effect on my forecast might be. The length of such an exercise would not only add greatly to an already lengthy discussion but also would not add much to my argument. Even if it were possible to specify *now* the range of all unexpected future events in order to make a good many forecasts, those forecasts would be of little use, except to tell us that almost anything could happen (which is, of course, one forecast, but not a very useful one). The art of forecasting really consists of

economy (the amount and types of inputs required to obtain given outputs), the Chinese policy of emphasizing self-dependency and not seeking or accepting long-term foreign loans or aid, and the stability of the leadership and its economic policies.

The rather slow growth in agriculture and the reduction of the relatively high growth rates in industry are derived from the assumption that there will be a downward trend in the productivity of inputs for these sectors, as a whole, over the next 15 years. This assumption is solidly grounded in both economic reasoning and historical evidence, not only for China but for other economies as well. The considerable time lag and investment that would be required for the spread and implementation of innovations that would lead to dramatic advances in the economic development problem would rule out any sudden change in the quantitative relationships between inputs and the outputs they produce (i.e., sudden jumps in productivity due to technological change) in different parts of China's economy. Furthermore, the relative neglect by the Chinese of the basic research and development efforts that lead to these innovations and their reliance on more traditional or "borrowed" sources of increased productivity would argue against any sudden technological transformation. Even were a miracle new seed to be developed, as was the case in the breakthrough that paved the way for the Green Revolution, it would still need reliable and adequate

---

selecting from that set of *possible* forecasts the one most *probable*, given our present knowledge, and this is exactly what I have tried to do in the preceding sections of this chapter.

Yet other critics—indicating that I have succeeded in doing what I have tried to do—argue that my forecast and its derivation appear so plausible and reasonable that they find it hard to believe that the forecast will actually "come true." Again, their attitude reflects a misunderstanding of what a forecast is: the estimate of future events on the basis of *present* knowledge, with the full knowledge that other unexpected or unpredictable future events *will occur* which will require revisions in the forecast. The attempt to include the unexpected or unpredictable within the derivation of my forecast, therefore, is by definition inconsistent. Rather, in subsequent sections of this study, I will discuss the possible effects of alternative, yet plausible, future events, i.e., those that are neither totally unexpected nor improbable and that would alter my forecast.

sources of water. Finally, the assumptions concerning the quantitative relationship between inputs and outputs reflect a consensus among China specialists that the Chinese are now in a much more difficult phase in achieving further expansion of their economy.

The pressure on domestic resources in face of the pace of expansion, of course, could be alleviated if the Chinese were to seek and accept large-scale foreign loans and aid. I have assumed that they will not adopt this policy and thus will have to maintain balance between exports and imports over the next 15 years. This assumption includes the possibility that short-term credit (up to five years) might be used in making payments for specific imports. However, it does not incorporate any intergovernmental loans or aid transfers that would enter the Chinese budget as a supplement to domestic revenue and add to the state's holding of foreign exchange. I believe this latter possibility is not very likely in light of China's history before 1949 and its experience with Soviet loans in the 1950s, Peking's very strong statements against such loans, and the commonly held belief that such loans and aid involve the anathema of either explicit or implicit ties and dependence. In addition, even if the Chinese sought these loans and aid, it would be very difficult for most Western industrialized countries to offer and extend them because of both political implications and institutional restrictions. Finally, unless the Chinese experience a serious economic crisis sometime during the next 15 years, they are likely to make slow but steady progress toward most of their economic objectives, which would over time reduce the pressure for seeking intergovernmental loans and aid—just as it has since the 1950s.

The more relevant question is whether or not the Chinese will seek and receive long-term commercial loans to finance large-scale, complete plants purchased abroad. Although the possibility of such a policy and its implications for this forecast are discussed in the next chapter, the forecast in Table 1 is based on a policy of no long-term loans, either intergovernmental or commercial. During the last few years, when the Chinese signed a large number of contracts to import complete plants, and price changes on the world market left them incurring sizable and increasing import surplusses, they extended some feelers concerning the possibility of long-term commercial loans. Nonetheless, current trade returns show that they have reacted to their balance-of-payments problem by bringing imports into line with export earnings and thus adhering to their principle of maintaining a balanced *total* trade. Furthermore, there is no indication that any group that may emerge victorious from the leadership struggle advocates a change in this policy. This small likelihood that the Chinese will seek long-term commercial loans from abroad in the near future is thus one of several reasons why Peking is extremely unlikely, to say the least, to allow for direct foreign investment in China's economy. In fact, the internal debate now centers on whether even the current level of commercial trade undermines the policy of self-dependence.

The possibilities that the Chinese will adopt any of these alternative economic policies could be significantly changed if either the radicals or the moderates were to emerge as the sole survivors in the current leadership struggle, which has intensified now that Mao has gone "to meet Marx." Thus, I am most uneasy about the crucial assumption that the "consensus" leadership of the radicals and moderates, who have argued about *relative* policy differences and not about complete or drastic institutional and policy changes in the past, will continue over the next 15 years. Nonetheless, this "consensus" leadership seems likely to prevail, since the basic boundaries and guidelines that will shape future economic institutions, policies, and decisions making appear already to have evolved from the struggles of the past 25 years. The arguments now taking place within the leadership group assume that these boundaries and guidelines will endure and really involve changes of degree and emphasis within them.

The possibility that an entirely new leadership group, pursuing a different set of objectives and advocating a different economic system, will suddenly emerge and overthrow the Peking regime therefore appears highly unlikely, at least over the next 15 years. Furthermore, the chances of success for either radical or moderate extremists among the current leaders also are highly unlikely since the extremists lack broad support in the Chinese political, economic, military, and social systems. If either extreme faction were in fact to succeed, its dominance of the leadership would nonetheless be quite unstable and undoubtedly would be temporary.

Yet political developments in China are much more difficult than economic developments to forecast, and the assumption of political stability is the most crucial to my economic forecast. Therefore, the following chapter will assess the implications of alternative political leadership and economic policies.

FIVE

Economic Influences on China's Future World Role

The cause-and-effect relationships or interactions between internal economic developments and a country's international relations and foreign policies are much too complicated and little understood to be investigated in this essay. The fact that my analysis of the probable evolution of China's economy over the next 15 years precedes the discussion of the effects that evolution may have on China's international relations should not be interpreted as an implicit assumption that economic developments are the cause and the resulting international relations are the effect. Although there are no general-equilibrium, theoretical models that identify and specify the nexus of causal relationships between internal economic developments and a country's international relations, it is clear that cause-and-effect relationships run in both directions, with changes in either area inducing changes in the other. Indeed, this essay is not intended to estimate China's role in the international system, taking into account all the factors—economic and political, both domestic and international—that will determine it.[1] It assumes that China's economic development over the next 10 to 15 years will be an important aspect of that determination, and in this chapter it seeks merely to analyze *which* features of China's development will be most influential, if not necessarily determinate.

[1] For an estimate of China's future role in the international system, taking all these factors into account, see Allen Whiting's essay in this volume.

The two most important of these characteristics are (1) the probability that the Chinese will achieve moderate, yet stable and steady, growth and (2) the ever-present threat that economic gains will be undermined by instability from any of a number of sources. Both these characteristics will strongly influence Peking to try to achieve stability in its future international relations and foreign policy. The rationale for this conclusion can best be understood through an examination of how the *threat* of economic instability and of the economic losses that instability would entail will be countered and constrained by the influence of powerful interest groups—persons within the political leadership, the masses, the economic planners, and the military—desiring to preserve stability in China's foreign relations.

POLITICAL LEADERSHIP AND POLICY CHANGES

The greatest threat to the stability of China's future economic evolution is the continuing struggle for control over the formulation and implementation of policy which permeates the political and administrative systems. This struggle between those favoring a more structural and moderate approach to China's economic, social, and political problems (within the basic context of a socialist revolution) and those favoring a more innovative and radical approach has plagued China's economic development since 1949.[2] Fortunately, these rival interest groups have at most times been able to work out meaningful compromises that go a long way toward explaining China's successful record over the past 25 years.[3]

[2] Many readers will disagree with the labeling and grouping of the wide variety of interest groups that have debated policy issues over the past 25 years into radicals and moderates. In reviewing all those debates, however, I cannot think of a more appropriate and meaningful set of labels reflecting the points of view of the protagonists. Since these terms represent a point of view rather than particular individuals or a particular program, they have not been capitalized.

[3] There are those observers, of course, who believe that China's success is due to Mao's belief in a "two-step forward, one-step backward" strategy of economic development. While this policy *may have been* necessary for keeping

At other times, these compromises have broken down and had serious consequences for the goals of either economic development or the socialist revolution. For example, the radical campaign to achieve a great leap into full socialism in 1958 may well have cost the Chinese a decade in economic growth. When the moderates gained control almost by default after the failure of the great-leap strategy, their economic programs did achieve economic restoration and growth in the early 1960s, but that very success seriously threatened to undermine some of the basic goals of the Chinese socialist revolution. The resulting backlash unleashed by the radicals in the Cultural Revolution of the mid-1960s, especially the much greater emphasis on self-sufficiency, also soon ran into trouble. Thus, a new consensus between moderate and radical policies emerged in 1970 and continued until the death of Chou En-lai in January 1976.

Chou En-lai was one of the most impressive men of the twentieth century. Almost no one could challenge his dedication to the socialist revolution in China or equal his political and administrative ability to realize its goals. Chou's unique but vital ability to act as Premier over the past several years and to accommodate, mediate between, and conciliate both radicals and moderates while still pursuing relatively moderate and stable, but successful, domestic and foreign policies served as a gyroscope for China's socialist revolution. Chou, of course, was not the only able political leader in China; able leaders could be found in the ranks of the radical and moderate camps at all levels of China's political system. Yet Chou appreciated the need for stability in both domestic and foreign relations and was able to achieve a compromise within the leadership in support of those policies.

His continued leadership would have done much to increase

---

alive and maintaining progress toward the ultimate goals of socialism, the evidence of the past 25 years does not support the argument that it is a successful policy of economic development. Nonetheless, even though this argument *may be* important for understanding developments over the past 25 years, as I have argued in the previous section of this study and do even more so in this section, such a policy in the future would have devastating consequences for the success of China's economic development: the risks are rising as China modernizes.

the probability that the Chinese would attain the level of economic growth over the next 15 years which was forecast above. His death suddenly created a vacuum in the political leadership which quickly led to a reemergence of the struggle throughout the political system between the radical and moderate points of view. Chou's handpicked successor, Teng Hsiao-p'ing, was a moderate who had lost political power during the Cultural Revolution. Having been helped back into a position of leadership by Chou, Teng served as acting Premier during Chou's confinement in the hospital but did not last long after Chou's death. Teng's problem, as it is with most other moderates, was his explicit advocacy and pursuit of moderate and "rational" economic programs for the sake of efficiency and material gains in the short run, combined with his lip service to the long-run socialist goals, and his unwillingness or inability to accommodate or reach compromises with the more radical elements of the leadership.

The ouster of Teng, however, signaled not a victory by the radicals but only a temporary prevention of a take-over by the moderates while an attempt was being made to work out a new compromise leadership. The death of Mao, coming as it did in the midst of these efforts, created a new leadership crisis in which the most powerful radicals apparently tried to take advantage of Mao's death to gain control of the government. That attempt failed when the four radical leaders on the Central Committee were arrested and other radicals were reportedly purged from positions of power. At the present time, Mao's handpicked successor, Hua Kuo-feng, appears to have weathered the crisis and to be firmly in control as China's new Premier. While the ultimate outcome of the current political struggle in China remains unpredictable, there are three very important reasons to believe that the Chinese—especially after the purge of the "Shanghai radicals"—will continue to pursue "compromise" leadership and to implement the moderate and stable domestic and foreign policies of the early 1970s.

The first reason is that the division between moderate and radical points of view is extensive and deep-seated. The range of effective policy options is not determined simply by who happens to be Premier, and it cannot be changed merely by removing the representative of one group and substituting that of another. Such changes at the top will influence the resulting policy decisions but will not change the fundamental beliefs and behavior of the participants from all classes in the Chinese political and administrative system. Furthermore, both moderate and radical leaders at the apex of these political and administrative systems have considerable and broadly based support. As China's experience over the past 25 years clearly indicates, any attempt to swing the center of gravity in political decision making completely to one extreme or the other would involve a traumatic purge of opponents at all levels. Such an attempt would likely prove unsuccessful, and it would obviously require open conflict that would directly threaten the success of the socialist revolution in China. This course would not be in the best interests of either group. Thus, consensus politics, or compromises between moderates and radicals, would appeal to their enlightened self-interest, although an attempt by either group to oust the other from power cannot be ruled out as a possibility over the next 15 years.[4]

A second factor that makes a continuation of compromise

[4]The argument in this paragraph relies on the assumption that representation of the moderate and radical points of view is approximately equal at each level of the political and administrative system. I have used this assumption merely for the purpose of arguing why the probability of a radical take-over and the resulting adoption of radical policies would undercut the possibility not only of stable economic growth but also of the maintenance of stable international relations as well. Although not an expert on Chinese politics, I believe the evidence indicates that the strength of the radical point of view increases as one moves from the local level to the apex of the political and administrative system and (without Mao) is not dominant, even at the top, which makes the possibility of a radical take-over even less probable. The ultimate outcome of the Cultural Revolution provides, I believe, ample evidence to support this view, as do the recent reports concerning the purge of the radicals.

My argument for the desire of both groups to avoid open conflict, i.e., riots and bloody confrontations in the streets, relies on their strenuous efforts to avoid these confrontations in the past 25 years, their skillful reliance on and ability to utilize compromise politics, and the much more probable recourse to "quiet," or "in-house," purges to secure domination, once one of these two groups has achieved what it believes is sufficient power to do so. Nonetheless, current reports from China indicate that the purge of the radicals may have broken out into open conflict in some regions.

politics seem likely is that China's leaders have been, in fact, attempting to avoid open conflicts, such as the riots in Peking following the death of Chou En-lai. The most important leader who did this was Mao himself. When Teng, an uncompromising advocate of the moderate point of view, was rejected as unacceptable by the radicals and their titular leader, Mao, uncompromising advocates of the radical point of view were passed over in the choice of his successor, Hua Kuo-feng. Not much is known of Hua's politics, but it is apparent that he was selected, with Mao's blessing, for the inevitable task of formulating a new leadership coalition dominated by neither radicals nor moderates. Hua's status and the possibility of accomplishing this task have been enhanced since the purge of the radical leaders. Although this argument involves considerable speculation, the new leadership group seems to be dominated by the moderates, whose strength may weaken both the forces opposing revisionism and the immediacy of the radicals' long-run social and political goals. Moreover, those radicals who might continue to play a role in China's leadership are likely to be those who realize that an immediate implementation of their preferred programs not only is politically impossible but also would subvert the leadership's efforts to achieve economic development.[5] Quite simply, developments since Mao's death significantly reduce the threat of instability in China's economic evolution which could result from a take-over by the radicals.

[5]One example—but only one of many such examples—of this dilemma in the radical point of view and of the radicals' explicit recognition of its existence is their argument over equality of income. The long-run goal is an equitable distribution of income, and the radicals are continually opposed to the introduction of institutional means for the distribution of incomes which will either perpetuate the inequities in the existing distribution of income or make them worse. Yet they recognize that the unequitable distribution of income (within industry, between industry and agriculture, between urban and rural areas, etc.) does exist in China and that an attempt to eliminate those inequalities overnight would destroy incentives and be counterproductive. The solution: continuous discussion and debate to keep the ultimate goal alive and slow, modest institutional changes, where possible, to move continuously toward that goal. The problem: impatience and poor judgment as to what institutional changes are possible and uncertainty as to how quickly those changes should be implemented.

Finally, a third factor—economic necessity—argues overwhelmingly, I believe, for the likelihood that compromise politics will be pursued. Quite simply, economic necessity has been the greatest obstacle to the radical cause over the past 25 years. Whenever radicals did gain control of the decision-making process and attempted to implement their programs, economic activity soon reacted unfavorably. In the face of these developments, the Chinese leadership—radicals and moderates alike—has revealed a remarkable flexibility and willingness to revert to more moderate policies to restore stability and growth. Thus, even if the radicals were to emerge victorious from the current leadership struggle and implement another great leap or cultural revolution, the harmful impact of those policies on the economy would encourage a rapid restoration of the economy to its equilibrium growth path.

The above arguments are presented largely to argue against the possibility of a complete take-over for an extended period of time by either the radical or the moderate forces during the next 15 years. Neither these arguments nor the forecast for the economy presented in Table 1 are meant to imply that there will be consistently stable growth rates or consensus leadership over that same period. Quite the contrary, the economic forecast summarized in Table 1 explicitly allows for short-run swings or deviations from the projected 15-year trend. These short-run deviations will depend largely on the cyclical behavior in agricultural production (resulting largely from changes in weather conditions) and on the effects of short-run changes in economic policy. In other words, the assumption of "consensus" political leadership with moderate economic policies, in general, over the next 15 years also allows for a continuation of fluctuation between periods of *relatively* more radical leadership and *relatively* more moderate leadership, with accompanying shifts in economic policy. In fact, the cycle in economic growth will be partially responsible for the changes in the center of gravity within the leadership; the latter changes, in turn, will affect the economic cycle.

As can be readily seen from the above, I do not assign a very high probability to a radical takeover, which has become even less likely in light of the events following Mao's death. Unfortunately, however, the threat of instability and economic crisis resulting from political struggles among China's leaders will continue to lurk in the shadows.

SOLUTION OF THE POPULATION-FOOD PROBLEM

The threat of instability is, however, diminishing considerably as China's economic development continues and its population gains a stake and interest in the continuation of stable growth. A major source of support for China's radical revolutionaries over the past 25 years has been their honest dedication to the cause of the masses. In agriculture, a very thorough land reform program gave the peasants land; when they were mobilized into collectivized agriculture an attempt was made to ensure that their income increased in order to prove the benefits of socialism over capitalism. In this respect, Chinese collectivization differed significantly from Stalin's. Rationing was introduced as much to ensure the equitable distribution of necessities as to restrict total consumption. And a wide dissemination of benefits accruing from health, education, and welfare expenditures, although still limited, remains a priority. There can be little doubt that China's leaders have attempted to provide the average Chinese with a "decent" and stable standard of living whose level and stability compare very favorably to those of the pre-1949 period.

Yet the most significant gains in this standard of living occurred in the early 1950s, and increases since then have been neither steady nor remarkable. Furthermore, the introduction of radical programs in the past has resulted rather quickly in serious problems for China's consumers, thus encouraging them to make an obvious connection between radical policies and lower standards of living. Exhortations to toil for the social good or for future material benefits have obtained brief periods of strenuous and dedicated efforts by the labor force; however, for more than a decade many of these campaigns have not led to significant improvements in the standard of living, and the pent-up demand for higher quality and increased amounts of both private *and* public consumption can be expected to take their toll unless satisfied. It is true that compared with the labor force in most capitalist and even other socialist countries, the Chinese today are motivated by a remarkably high level of cooperative spirit and social purpose. Nonetheless, the demand for an even higher standard of living is growing, fed in part by what the economic lexicon calls the "demonstration effect" within China itself—good housing and clothing or relatively high incomes and standards of living can be seen by all to exist, but remain inaccessible for much of the population in most areas. This demonstration effect is made even more evident to the peasant through the small-scale-industry program, which significantly increases the income of the rural areas where factories are located, of the workers who are assigned to work in those industries, and of the residents of the emerging urban centers where these industries are clustered.

Despite the attempt to implant true socialist values and behavior in the average Chinese, more income still yields more material benefits, which in turn satisfy basic needs such as food, clothing, and housing. Stable growth, i.e., moderate economic policies, directly benefits these materialistic aspirations of the Chinese consumer. Redistribution can be a solution only when there are significantly unequal incomes to be redistributed, a condition that no longer exists in China. People who have succeeded over the past two decades in earning a higher income within the relatively narrow range of inequitable distribution have done so on the basis of their skills and efforts; this significant portion of the labor force is becoming an important interest group. Both these relatively well-off consumers, whose success has been made possible by conditions created by Peking, and those who still aspire to gain relatively high standards of living would pose a serious obstacle to new attempts to institute radical economic policies. It is the hope of the radicals, of course, to "educate" and "reeducate" this potential force of revisionism, but the force is there and will grow stronger as economic growth continues.

The most serious problem faced by the Chinese consumer is the rationing of food. As argued earlier in this study, the Chinese are unlikely to solve their agricultural problem over the next 15 years and, even if successful in reducing the rate of population growth, will need to rely on imports of foodstuffs to close the gap between supply and the rationed demand. Furthermore, the gap might grow in absolute terms. Chinese consumers, especially those in the northern urban centers, thus have a vested interest in these imports. In other words, the solution to China's population-food problem over the next 15 years will increasingly depend on the ability of the Chinese to develop stable and friendly relations with foreign suppliers of foodstuffs, especially grain.

Several other considerations regarding China's demand for large-scale imports of foodstuffs must be taken into account as influences on China's future role in the international order. The estimates in Chapter Four concerning China's inability to solve the agricultural problem assumed that relatively normal weather conditions would prevail over the next 15 years. Two to three years of severe weather in certain regions—periods that have occurred frequently in Chinese history— could easily cause a serious agricultural crisis that would spread to other sectors of the economy and disrupt stable and balanced growth. While it is difficult to predict the political and foreign policy implications of such a crisis, a significant move to more moderate domestic policies and even greater dependence on foreign suppliers of food supplies and loans would seem likely. In the event of a truly serious crisis, however, the threat of domestic political turmoil and radical take-over could eventuate in greater instability and hostility in China's foreign relations. In addition, attempts by "hostile" neighbors to take advantage of China's turmoil and economic crises also must be considered a possibility. The likelihood of these unfavorable developments is not very great, however.

Another unfavorable outcome of China's population-food problem is even less likely. In the 1950s, a popular argument depicted China as solving its population-food crises by seizing and occupying surplus food areas on its borders. A serious agricultural crisis in the future presumably would increase the likelihood that China would resort to this solution. These arguments were not persuasive in the 1950s; developments since then have made them even less compelling. There are few, if any, easily accessible surplus agricultural areas on China's borders. In addition, over the past 25 years China's behavior along the border has been very defensive. Even when the Chinese achieved remarkable and sudden success in the Sino-Indian Border War, they withdrew their troops quickly in favor of negotiating a settlement. Also, the Chinese now face a concentration of a hostile neighbor's well-equipped troops along its northern boundaries, the longest land border in the world. Thus, a military adventure in South Asia during a Chinese agricultural crisis can be ruled out as contrary to a basic aim of China's foreign and military policy.

Nonetheless, even if weather conditions did not induce an agricultural crisis during the next 15 years, they might be severe enough to make the maintenance of even a 2 percent annual rate of growth in agricultural production difficult. If this were the case, the import demand for foodstuffs could be even larger than I anticipate. Already one of the world's largest importers of food grains, China could easily find itself the dominant buyer in a very tight sellers' market, competing with not only its major rival in the socialist camp but other less developed countries as well. In this situation, the Chinese would be under great pressure not only to follow peaceful and cooperative foreign relations and to expand trade relations with the major Western suppliers of food grains but also to consider foreign long-term loans and even aid as a means of easing their economic problems.[6]

Finally, most of the above discussion uses this study's rather modest estimates of future growth in agricultural production as a basic frame of reference. Undoubtedly, some China experts would view the future prospects with more optimism. There is indeed a possibility that yields will increase more rapidly than I have suggested because of either very favorable weather, which

[6]As will be discussed below, similar pressure will come from the need to import modern technology in support of their industrialization efforts over the next 15 years; a serious agricultural crisis would merely shift this pressure from the need to obtain capital goods to the need to obtain foodstuffs. Nonetheless, the recent United States agreement to supply India with food grains at cheap prices for 5 percent down, with the remainder financed by a long-term loan, repayment to begin in 10 years, would appear very appealing, despite well-entrenched ideological and political opposition in China's leadership, and would be hard to resist in the midst of a serious agricultural crisis.

is most unlikely, or a more rapid pace than anticipated in the spread of irrigation, new seeds, rice cultivation, etc. If agricultural production were to grow annually by 3 percent rather than by 2 percent, both higher standards of living and a more rapid rate of investment and industrialization would be possible. Equally important, the need for imports of producer goods to support the more rapid pace of industrialization would be increased. Under these more optimistic conditions over the next 15 years, which I believe are possible but not probable, most of the above arguments would continue to hold: the gains for both China's political leaders and consumers that would be obtained from continued stable growth would enhance the tendency toward moderate domestic and foreign policies.

Nonetheless, if the economic results were so successful that the rather tight constraints imposed by agricultural development on China's export capacity, rate of investment, and standard of living were considerably alleviated, the possibility of another radical great leap to achieve in the short run the ultimate goals of socialism would increase. Yet the foregoing arguments should demonstrate that the Chinese are very unlikely to solve their agricultural problem over the next 15 years and that their domestic and foreign policies will probably not become dominated by radicalism.

TRADE POLICY

Several interest groups favor developing trade relations with Western nations. One, the Chinese consumers (especially in the northern urban area), developed only after food grains supplied by Western nations became an important supplement to China's total grain supply in the 1960s. Another important interest group that favors developing trade relations with Western industrialized countries—the economic planners and managers—has had an interest in maintaining foreign trade relations since the creation of the People's Republic of China in 1949. Yet the radical point of view, which argues for a self-dependent approach to China's economic development and a "limitation" of China's dependence on foreign sources of supply, is accepted by most Chinese leaders as a long-run policy guideline. Nonetheless, China's economic development during the 1950s, a period of rapid growth rates, depended on sizable imports of producer goods from the socialist countries. In a separate study, using the empirical evidence provided by China's foreign trade behavior, I have shown that only for a brief period following the Cultural Revolution (1966–1969) did the Chinese actively pursue a policy of self-dependence with a resulting decline in imports of producer goods.[7] Since the reemergence of moderate control over economic policies in 1970, the growth in imports of producer goods and in the signing of contracts for the delivery of complete plants has been remarkable. Notwithstanding the often repeated emphasis on self-sufficiency, the actual embodiment of that slogan in the current program of developing small-scale industry in rural areas throughout the countryside, and the role of that policy in stemming a wholesale reliance on the "blind" borrowing of foreign models and expertise, the last 25-year period as a whole in fact represents one of the most prominent examples ever of a country's relying on imported producer goods and foreign technology to achieve domestic industrialization.

Today, even the rural, small-scale industrial program is sustained by modern technology, machinery, and equipment. Since China's industrialization efforts of the past 25 years have made the country relatively self-sufficient in many producer goods, many of these needs are provided for by its large-scale, modern sector or its rural, small-scale industrial sector rather than by "native" technology, i.e., equipment made by the local blacksmith. Nonetheless, the large-scale, modern industrial sector still relies directly on imported producer goods. The economic planners and managers of that sector realize the vital role that foreign trade plays in assuring the continued growth of

[7]Robert F. Dernberger, "Economic Development and Modernization in Contemporary China," forthcoming in *Technology and Communist Culture*, Praeger Publishers.

traditional as well as new industries; in this sense, China's current foreign trade behavior fully illustrates the sizable needs for machinery and equipment from abroad. Over the next 15 years, however, China's industrialization efforts also will require major imports of metals, especially iron and steel.

Foreign trade will also be vitally important in providing for continued imports of chemical fertilizer that will be needed to achieve the rate of growth forecast for agriculture. When the 13 new fertilizer complexes purchased in the West go into production in 1980, the Chinese should become self-sufficient in the production of nitrogenous fertilizer and imports of fertilizer can be expected to remain relatively stable.

Thus, the forecast for China's economic growth and standard of living over the next 15 years relies on significant imports of food grains, producer goods (and technology), chemical fertilizers, and metals. In other words, it depends on the maintenance and further development of stable commercial trade and, therefore, political relations with foreign countries, especially the industrialized and agricultural surplus nations in the Western world. But why the Western world? Why not the socialist bloc of industrialized countries? This question, which has important implications for China's future role in the international order, is raised below. Before attempting an answer, however, it should be noted that economic developments in China over the past decade— particularly the discovery and exploitation of its vast petroleum reserves—have significantly changed the nature of China's choices regarding its policy of limited reliance on foreign trade. This development alone is likely to lead the Chinese economic planners and managers to advocate the development of stable and normal foreign trade relations, *even in the absence* of a vital need for imports of food grains, producer goods, chemical fertilizer, and metals.

Development of Petroleum Resources

Over the past decade, the production of crude oil in China has increased annually by 25 percent; onshore and offshore recoverable reserves are conservatively estimated to be, respectively, 20 billion and 30 billion barrels.[8] Concurrent with this rapid development of domestic production, imports were phased out as a source of supply in the mid-1960s, and China began to export modest amounts of oil. By the mid-1970s, the Chinese were exporting over 5 million tons of oil, mostly to Japan. During the next 15 years, therefore, China's exports of oil would appear to offer a ready solution to its severe balance-of-payments problems. (In the mid-1970s China's imports have been exceeding its exports, and in 1974 the import surplus was as great as 1 billion U.S. dollars.) This balance-of-payments problem will continue unless imports are reduced, exports are increased, or the Chinese seek long-term loans or aid from abroad. Since crude oil is a commodity in great demand in the world market, many foreign observers believe that the continued development of China's oil production will not simply mitigate these balance-of-payments constraints but actually eliminate them.

There is reason for being cautious in this regard, however. As a developing country, China can expect the domestic demand for energy supplies to rise relatively rapidly over the next 15 years; this is especially true for oil, inasmuch as the Chinese are likely to shift to a relatively greater use of oil, diesel fuel, and gasoline as sources of energy.[9] Because of this increasing demand, one estimate holds that even under the most favorable assumptions, China will be able to export annually over the next decade or so no more than one-tenth of the oil exported by OPEC in 1974; according to that study, a more reasonable estimate would be about one-twentieth.[10] In fact, given the potential for industrialization and the vast size of the country, which requires an extensive and well-developed transportation network, China's reliance on oil as a major source of foreign exchange could diminish quickly if domestic demand soon exceeded the available supply.

[8]Selig S. Harrison, "Time Bomb in East Asia," *Foreign Policy*, no. 20, Fall, 1975, pp. 5–6.

[9]Between 1970 and 1974, oil increased its share in China's total energy supply from 14 to 22 percent.

[10]CIA, *China: Energy Balance Projections*, A(ER)75-75, November 1975, p. 18.

Moreover, growth rates of 20 to 25 percent in the oil industry will be difficult to maintain over the next 15 years. The attempt to recover the offshore reserves not only will be costly but also will involve a considerable time lag. To tap the potential of these oil reserves, the Chinese will need both drilling facilities and means for transporting oil from the drill head to either the domestic user or the ocean ports (which also need facilities for ocean tankers) for export. Even if the technology, equipment, and skilled workers were to be obtained from abroad, adding significantly to the demand for imports, these items are currently in scarce supply and would involve high costs and the direct involvement of foreign companies in China's development programs. Perhaps because of these reasons, the Chinese appear to have adopted a go-slow policy in developing their *exports* of petroleum, relying primarily on their own development of the necessary technology and equipment while utilizing piecemeal imports from abroad.

Finally, two other aspects of the world market for oil will have a significant effect on China's potential earnings from oil exports. In terms of quality, different Chinese oil fields are said to produce oil that suffers from (1) high freezing points (and thus cannot be used to fuel jets which fly at altitudes with very low temperatures) or (2) too low a flash point (which causes danger of fires) or (3) too high a viscosity (which means that the oil flows slowly and must be heated for transmission through pipelines) or (4) too high a sulfur content (which pollutes) or (5) too high a paraffin count (which increases the cost of refining).[11] Even if Chinese crude oil were found to be of very high quality, however, the recent world crisis in oil and the relatively high prices it created set off forces that can be expected to reduce the relative price of oil in the

[11] I am not a petroleum expert and have no knowledge concerning the validity of these claims or whether those who make them have any more expertise than myself. That explains the use of "are said to" in this sentence. Furthermore, the quality of Chinese oil depends on its origin. Shengli oil is of the lowest quality; Taching oil is low in sulfur but high in paraffin, etc. However valid these specific claims may be, modern uses of petroleum products require specific qualities in the crude oil used as a raw material or very costly refining processes for eliminating the undesirable qualities of the crude oil; most Western refineries are equipped to handle Middle Eastern oil which is high in sulfur but low in paraffin.

future. These include the development of new sources of supply, the switch to other sources of energy, and the development of technology that is "oil-saving." As this process develops, the pressures on OPEC, an unstable grouping of producers to begin with, should also significantly reduce cartel control over supply for the purpose of rigging prices in the international market.

Despite these words of caution, China's exploitation of its oil resources will provide it with an excellent export commodity that is in greatest demand in those very countries that can supply the Chinese with the imports they need. This development has made the economic planners and managers a very potent force favoring greater involvement in normal foreign trade activities. The reason is simple: The supply of oil in excess of the current needs of the domestic economy is valuable only as a commodity for foreign trade. It cannot be used as food or poured into molds and made into machines; it can, however, be shipped abroad in exchange for food grains, machines, technology, chemical fertilizers, etc. Thus, given China's potential supply of oil, both the costs of its policy of self-dependency and the gains that would result from normal trade relations with the industrialized and food-surplus countries of the West are very large.

Choice of Trading Partners

Another aspect of China's foreign trade that will continue to make the economic planners and managers a strong interest group in favor of normalized trade and diplomatic relations with the West is the inability of the socialist countries to supply the imports China needs and can get from the Western countries. The Soviet Union was a major supplier of producer goods during the 1950s, when China was rehabilitating and expanding basic industries that did not require sophisticated or advanced technology. Now and in the future, China will be able to supply *these* producer goods domestically; it needs instead producer goods that embody advanced technology. The socialist countries, although able to meet some of China's technological needs, are themselves currently seeking imports of these high-technology producer goods in the West. As far as chemical fertilizers and food grains are concerned, the advantage of the Western countries is even greater in comparison with the socialist countries.

Oil earns hard currency. To export it to the socialist countries, which use bilateral trade accounts, would tie those earnings to Chinese purchases from the socialist trading partner. Transport costs for trade with the socialist countries are also relatively high, especially when compared with transport costs for trade with Japan, China's largest trading partner. Finally, China's export commodities probably accommodate Japan's needs more than they do the needs of any other industrialized country; this allows for a much more balanced bilateral trade (which is not a necessity but is a desirable feature of foreign trade as far as the Chinese are concerned) than China can achieve with any other major trading partner or area in the West.

Although Japan's dominance as China's major trading partner will probably continue in the future, the Chinese also can be expected to follow a policy of diversifying their partners in foreign trade and avoiding exclusive dependence on any one country or group of countries. This policy will likely lead China to develop trade ties with all countries and areas: the socialist countries (including the Soviet Union), Japan, the industrialized countries of North America and Western Europe, agricultural-surplus countries in South America and Southeast Asia, and raw material suppliers among the ranks of the underdeveloped countries. This policy, in general, will be a favorable force for China's participation in an accommodating manner in the institutional order of the international system. At the same time, however, this development of alternative sources of supply will enable the Chinese to use foreign trade as a weapon of foreign policy, as they have in the past. Yet this threat is not as serious as popular journalistic reports would indicate; China's trade does not and will not account for a very significant share of its Western partners' total foreign trade. More important, China is neither the first nor the worst offender in using foreign trade to achieve other goals of its foreign policy. In fact, Chinese behavior over the past 25 years shows a remarkable willingness to play the game by the rules. China has more often than not been the victim rather than the victor when it has tried to influence a foreign country's domestic or foreign policies through foreign trade threats.

Foreign Long-Term Loans and Aid

The above discussion argues that actual developments in China's foreign trade over the next 15 years, by their very nature, will result in considerable pressure on China's leaders to cooperate in both the development of an institutional order and the search for solutions to the problems the world will face. Indeed, foreign trade can provide China with a means to alleviate or overcome both the constraints on economic growth and the effects of natural or man-made disruptions. In this respect, long-term loans and foreign aid would have a very high *economic* benefit to China's economic planners and managers.

Reliance on Soviet loans during the early 1950s—Moscow gave Peking almost no outright foreign aid—was not only an economic necessity; it was also deemed ideologically and politically acceptable by the Chinese leadership as exemplifying socialist brotherly love and selfless assistance. The Chinese themselves extend foreign aid and loans to less developed nations, both socialist and nonsocialist, in their attempt to counter Soviet and Western efforts to win friends among and influence the political leaders and peoples of those countries. Because China well realizes its own purposes in this area and has experienced Moscow's attempt to use its assistance as a lever on Chinese domestic and foreign policy, the Chinese over the past 15 years have been rigidly opposed to large-scale or long-term borrowing from abroad and adamant about not seeking foreign aid. In this respect, they have indeed maintained a strict policy of self-dependency and are a rare example of a developing country, either historically or in the contemporary world, that is a creditor nation with an excellent credit rating.

Notwithstanding ideological and political matters, the Chinese—in light of their relatively firm central control over the domestic economy and society and their relative ability to secure defense capabilities from external manipulation—are most likely to avail themselves of the tremendous economic advantages offered by low-cost and long-term commercial loans over the next 15 years. These commercial loans will be made by foreign enterprises, banks, or consortiums and undoubtedly will be tied to the imports of particular commodities, including complete plants. Large-scale, long-term intergovernmental loans or foreign aid can be expected to remain outside the pale of Chinese foreign trade policy, perhaps because of a fear that such loans would open the Chinese to direct or indirect meddling by other governments in their economy. Nonetheless, the reliance on commercial loans rather than intergovernmental loans will still require the Chinese to maintain their credit rating on the international money market, and this will encourage their participation in the future international system.

The extent to which the Chinese will rely on these commercial loans is likely to be rather limited, which is consistent with the forecast for China's economic growth. Yet greater reliance on commercial loans could conceivably enable the Chinese to achieve substantial economic gains, such as increases in the rate of growth or the alleviation of constraints placed by slow growth on other domestic objectives. The attractiveness to the Chinese of borrowing foreign funds in a manner that would enable them to retain control over the use of the imports they finance and the desire of foreign suppliers to provide these loans to facilitate sales to the Chinese make it possible, although not likely, that China may borrow abroad to such an extent that it could become a significant debtor country during the next 15 years. If this were to happen, the additional loans would finance an equivalent increase in the level of imports; depending upon what sorts of commodities were imported, the Chinese might achieve higher rates of growth in agricultural and industrial output and in the standard of living than those forecast in Table 1.

These developments would have several consequences for China's role in the international system. The greater level of dependence on commercial loans from abroad, the increased amounts of imports in the Chinese economic development program, and the readily identifiable economic gains provided by both would be a strong force for the greater integration of the Chinese into the international system. However, as argued earlier in this study, increased economic success would increase the possibility that the center of gravity in leadership and economic policies would shift in favor of the radicals. Finally, economic gains would increase the demands of the masses for higher standards of living. On balance, however, Peking's willingness alone to engage in long-term commercial borrowing on such a scale would be a clear indication that its attitude had shifted significantly in favor of greater integration; the economic results obtained from this policy would strongly reinforce that change in attitude.

MILITARY STRATEGY

Mao openly criticized those who desired to rely on modern weaponry, especially those who advocated dependence on Soviet help in modernizing China's military. He argued that modern weapons systems were orientated to *offensive* military strategy, whereas China's needs were for a *defensive* military strategy and capacity that could rely upon the strength of the masses. A review of China's military strategy over the past 25 years does, in fact, suggest that it has been oriented toward defense rather than offense. Such a review also indicates that the military has been a focal point in the contest between the radical and moderate points of view; the former has frequently won that debate, which has resulted in the purge of those military leaders who argued openly and strongly for the modernization or professionalization of China's military forces. Nonetheless, given the nature of China's actual military engagements over the past 25 years and the military capabilities of its potential enemies, those who are responsible for Chinese military performance in conflicts that may occur over the next 10 to 15 years undoubtedly appreciate the role that modern weapons will play in determining the outcome.

In a study of the costs of military expenditures in China, I concluded that those costs would preclude the possibility of China's creating a military capacity equal to that of the superpowers.[12] Nonetheless, China can be expected, for the purpose of credibility, to continue its relatively limited

[12] Robert F. Dernberger, "The Economic Consequences of Defense Expenditure Choices in China," in *China: A Reassessment of the Economy*, pp. 467–498.

development of intermediate-range ballistic missiles with nuclear warheads. Although costly, this limited development of nuclear weaponry is possible within the bounds forecast for China's future economic growth, and it is desired by most members of the leadership.

Those charged with the responsibility of defending China's border can be expected to be a politically powerful interest group that favors or at least supports moderate economic policies as those most likely to assure China's continued economic development—especially the production of those items essential for the modernization of China's conventional weapons systems (e.g., mobile armored units, naval forces, and air power). The industries essential to assure this production would include the metal industries (high-grade finished metals and alloys), the machine-building industry (modern military equipment), the chemical industry, the fuel industry, the transportation industries, etc. These interest groups also would desire the development and maintenance of foreign trade relations that would help secure this economic growth. Inasmuch as neither Moscow nor Washington is likely to be a source for the military equipment itself or for the technology relevant to its domestic production, China's military leaders also desire that the development of China's own technical and research capabilities keep pace with military developments throughout the world. For example, the production of outdated MIGs, even on a large scale, would hardly give the Chinese air superiority against an enemy whose planes were equipped with air-to-air, heat-seeking missiles. As it has been in the past, the development of this technical and research capability would be threatened by the adoption of radical political and economic programs.

China's military leaders also have an interest in stable international relations which is equally as important as their interest in internal stability and pursuit of stable economic growth. China's present inability—even in defensive operations along its borders against a well-equipped opponent in either limited hostilities or a full-fledged invasion—to engage opponents on equal terms in mobile armored conflict, to gain superiority in the air to protect its own troops, or to hold its own in naval engagements may well increase the romantic appeal or political orthodoxy of relying on the masses to sustain guerrilla warfare, as in the Chinese civil war. But war is war, and China's military leaders remember well that the Korean conflict was not a guerrilla campaign, was fought with modern Soviet weapons, and was severely hampered by the lack of air cover. Similarly, the Quemoy crisis was not a guerrilla engagement and ended in a failure to achieve Chinese objectives. Perhaps the most important argument for China's interest in stable international relations, however, remains the visible concentration of Soviet troops on its borders. The Chinese know that their conventional weapons systems are not adequate to meet the Soviet threat, and they need time to make them more modern. China's military leadership is therefore likely to be a powerful interest group in support of moderate policies for economic growth domestically, the negotiation of China's grievances with hostile neighbors, and China's cooperative participation in efforts toward defusing international tensions.

* * * * *

Some readers may object to my use of "interest group" analyses in the determination of the influence of China's future economic development on China's role in the international system. But few could object to the identification of the political leadership, consumers, economic planners and managers, and the military as terribly important interest groups in China. The question is: How important are these groups in decision making and policy formulation? My analysis assumes not that these groups are active participants in decision making but only that their "interests" are an important element in the decision-making process. I believe that China's domestic and economic policies over the past 25 years clearly indicate that these interests have been considered in the decision-making process, which helps to explain the political leadership's success in maintaining control over the world's largest society. No matter how absolute or authoritarian or how dominated by a single person or group, policies formulated in Peking must be implemented throughout the political system if they are to achieve their objective; the compliance and support of each of these interest groups is essential for that purpose. Moreover, the leadership's function is largely one of problem solving: as social, political, and economic problems arise, leaders must react to them and also consider and respond to the pressures from these interest groups in determining policies.

However, one need not assume that the "enlightened" self-interest of China's leadership ensures concern for the interests of these groups in the formulation of policy. There is considerable evidence that China's leaders share those interests (which is important in explaining why they are China's leaders). Quite simply, China is not ruled by a small minority who seized power through a palace coup; it is ruled by one of the few communist parties in the world that seized power through armed struggle of the peasantry. The success of consensus rule is based less on shrewd manipulation or deception of the populace than on the strength of the political system that was introduced in 1949.

SIX

China's Role in the International System

The preceding analyses of China's likely economic development during the next 10 to 15 years are intended to provide a basis for forecasting China's likely role in the future international system. Thus, I have attempted to identify and analyze China's economic development and to suggest how certain characteristics may influence the pursuit of foreign economic and political relations. Since the length and scope of this study preclude a detailed discussion of either the specific form that the international system is likely to assume or the particular problems it is likely to encounter, my conclusions concerning China's role in that system must necessarily be somewhat general.

The evolution of China's economy—especially regarding both the probability of achieving modest, but relatively stable, rates of growth and the threat that instability from any number of sources may undermine economic gains—will influence Peking to adhere to what I have called a moderate, cooperative, or accommodative orientation in its international relations, for several reasons. As Chapter Five suggested, the pursuit of domestic economic growth would likely be impeded by disruptions in China's international relations. Agricultural growth—the greatest constraint on China's economic development—is unlikely to exceed an annual rate of 2 percent over the next 10 to 15 years; to feed its growing population, China will therefore require imports of foodstuffs whose availability will depend on stable relations with foreign suppliers. Similarly, China's economic planners and managers will continue to advocate the maintenance of foreign trade relations. Although the large-scale, modern industrial sector now supplies many of the producer goods needed for the rural, small-scale industrial sector, the modern sector still relies heavily on imported producer goods for its own needs. As the effort to industrialize continues, China will require major imports of metals and advanced technologies.

China's likely desire to avoid dependence on any one trading partner will probably increase the country's involvements with other nations. The discovery of petroleum reserves has significantly altered Peking's options concerning its policy of limited reliance on foreign trade. The trend toward integration would be enhanced if Peking accepts the likely advice of its economic planners and makes greater use of long-term commercial loans, a policy that would carry substantial economic benefits.

Other factors will also encourage moderate behavior. Although economic, military, and political development during the past 25 years have reinforced the role of the PRC as a major actor in world affairs, China remains less powerful than the two superpowers. China is unlikely to acquire the economic capabilities to become a superpower in the next 10 to 15 years. Moreover, relatively few countries (even in the Third World) lie within its sphere of influence. And these countries are so limited in terms of their ability to complement China's own military and political power that China's relative weakness in comparison with the superpowers is likely to lead Peking to pursue a moderate foreign policy as the most effective way of achieving its international objectives. More tangibly, the Soviet concentration of troops on the border will also encourage Peking to avoid conflict and instability.

Two general but important objections can be raised against my analysis. Each could mean a less forthcoming Chinese position in international affairs than my forecast would indicate. First, if my assumptions concerning interest-group analyses are not borne out, Peking would be less constrained than I have suggested to pursue a moderate and stable course of economic development that would entail friendly relations with other governments and a generally accommodative international posture. But as I indicated in the conclusion to Chapter Five, I believe that policies pursued during the last 25 years offer sufficient evidence that China's leaders are not only influenced by these interest groups but actually share the concerns of these groups as well.

Second, and perhaps more open to dispute, different assumptions of rates of growth could lead to dramatic divergences in conclusions about China's likely behavior. If the moderates are either very successful or very unsuccessful in achieving economic development, the challenge from the radicals can be expected to grow more potent. On the one hand, if the economic programs of the moderates achieve too low a rate of growth, the constraints on China's political behavior—both domestic and international— would increase. Sufficiently severe economic problems could discredit the economic program of the moderates and increase the appeal of the radicals' approach. On the other hand, a very high rate of growth of approximately 7 percent—even if sustained for only a few years—not only would significantly reduce the economic constraints on China's domestic and international political policy choices but also would likely strengthen the arguments of the radicals that the pace of China's social revolution should be quickened. In either case, the assumption of power by the radicals could well lead to instability in China's international relations.

The radical point of view is likely to remain an important force in Chinese politics, even after the death of Mao and the ensuing purge of radical leaders. Especially important in this regard is the radicals' insistence that although the social and political imperatives of certain moderate policies may be conducive to successful economic development, they actually threaten the long-run objectives of China's socialist revolution. Thus, even if the moderates' policies do succeed, the radicals are likely to challenge them continually. Nonetheless, these challenges are likely to be accompanied by a desire to avoid traumatic purges and open conflict.

These considerations make my conclusions concerning the impact of China's economic development on its foreign policy less than certain. In assessing China's role in the international system, it should be remembered that any assumptions of China's economic growth rate must be qualified by the possibility that external constraints ultimately may prove more important than the domestic economy in influencing Peking's choice of policies. Although economic pressures are likely to lead Peking to adopt an accommodative orientation toward the resolution of international problems, certain political and military security objectives may cause China to assume what some Western governments would call a nonaccommodative, or even hostile, position, even to the detriment of progress in its economic development. Events in several areas may be perceived by Peking as threatening China's self-interest and long-term goals. Chinese assertiveness, resulting in international instability, could be stimulated by what happens concerning Korea, Taiwan, Indochina, India-Pakistan, the Soviet Union, disarmament, rights to offshore oil, the international trade and finance system, and—to a lesser extent—the Middle East and the political evolution and integration into the world system of the less developed countries.

Whatever institutional framework and methods for problem solving develop in the world, one statement can be made with certainty: If the world is to be peaceful, that framework and those methods must provide for the participation of both China and the Soviet Union and must also facilitate a reduction in the hostility between the two countries. Ultimately, the behavior of the Chinese and of the Soviets themselves will determine whether or not that hostility is defused. Yet any system that perpetuates or reinforces the current tensions is highly unlikely to be stable.

Selected Bibliography

Bettleheim, Charles, *Cultural Revolution and Industrial Organization in China*, Monthly Review Press, New York, 1974.

Chen, Nai-ruenn, and Walter Galenson, *The Chinese Economy under Communism*, Aldine Publishing Company, Chicago, 1969.

China: A Reassessment of the Economy, a compendium of papers submitted to the Joint Economic Committee of the Congress of the United States, U.S. Government Printing Office, Washington, D.C., 1975.

Donnithorne, Audrey, *China's Economic System,* Praeger Publishers, Inc., New York, 1967.

Eckstein, Alexander, *China's Economic Development*, University of Michigan Press, Ann Arbor, Mich., 1975.

———, *China's Economic Revolution*, Cambridge University Press, New York, 1977.

An Economic Profile of Mainland China, a compendium of papers submitted to the Joint Economic Committee of the Congress of the United States, U.S. Government Printing Office, Washington, D.C., 1967.

Goodstadt, Leo, *China's Search for Plenty*, John Weatherhill, Inc., New York, 1973.

People's Republic of China: An Economic Assessment, a compendium of papers submitted to the Joint Economic Committee of the Congress of the United States, U.S. Government Printing Office, Washington, D.C., 1972.

Perkins, Dwight, *Market Control and Planning in Communist China*, Harvard University Press, Cambridge, Mass., 1966.

————, *Agricultural Development in China, 1368–1968*, Aldine Publishing Company, Chicago, 1969.

————, *China's Modern Economy in Historical Perspective*, Stanford University Press, Stanford, Calif., 1975.

————, Alexander DeAngelis, Robert F. Dernberger, et al., *Rural Small-Scale Industry in the People's Republic of China*, University of California Press, Berkeley, 1977.

Prybyla, Jan S., *The Political Economy of Communist China*, International Textbook, Scranton, Pa., 1970.

Richman, Barry M., *Industrial Society in Communist China*, Random House, New York, 1969.

Robinson, Joan, *Economic Management in China*, Modern China Series No. 4, Anglo-Chinese Educational Institute, London, 1975.

Wu, Yuan-li (ed.), *China: A Handbook*, Praeger Publishers, Inc., New York, 1973.

Index

About the Authors

ALLEN S. WHITING is a professor of political science and an associate of the Center for Chinese Studies at the University of Michigan. He headed the Office of Research and Analysis for the Far East in the State Department, 1962–1966, and was deputy consul general in Hong Kong, 1966–1968. He resided on Taiwan in 1953–1954 and in 1974–1975 and has travelled widely in the Soviet Union, China, Japan, and Southeast Asia. He has written or co-authored five books, including *China Crosses The Yalu: The Decision To Enter the Korean War* (Stanford University Press, 1968) and *The Chinese Calculus of Deterrence: India and Indochina* (University of Michigan Press, 1975).

ROBERT F. DERNBERGER is a professor of economics and an associate of the Center for Chinese Studies at the University of Michigan. He received a B.A. and M.A. in Far Eastern Studies at the University of Michigan and a Ph.D. in economics at Harvard University. While serving on the faculty of the University of Chicago, Professor Dernberger was Chairman of the University's Committee on Far Eastern Studies and editor of the University's journal, *Economic Development and Cultural Change*. He has written numerous papers on the economy of the People's Republic of China, including "The Role of The Foreigner in China's Economic Development, 1840–1949," in Dwight Perkins (ed.), *China's Economy in Historical Perspective,* (Stanford University Press, 1975) and "Radical Ideology and Economic Development in China: The Cultural Revolution and Its Impact on the Economy," *Asian Survey,* December 1972. Professor Dernberger is also co-author of the forthcoming book, *Rural Small-Scale Industry in The People's Republic of China* (University of California Press).

BAYLESS MANNING is the president of the Council on Foreign Relations.